HOLACRACY

HOLACRACY

THE NEW
MANAGEMENT SYSTEM
FOR A RAPIDLY
CHANGING WORLD

BRIAN J. ROBERTSON

Henry Holt and Company   New York

Henry Holt and Company, LLC
Publishers since 1866
175 Fifth Avenue
New York, New York 10010
www.henryholt.com

Henry Holt® and ® are registered trademarks
of Henry Holt and Company, LLC.

Library of Congress Cataloging-in-Publication Data

Robertson, Brian J.
  Holacracy : the new management system for a rapidly
changing world / Brian J. Robertson.—First edition.
    pages cm
  Includes bibliographical references and index.
  ISBN 978-1-62779-428-2 (hardcover)—ISBN 978-1-62779-429-9
(electronic book) 1. Delegation of authority. 2. Employee empowerment.
3. Management—Employee participation. 4. Organizational effectiveness.
5. Organizational behavior. I. Title.
  HD50.R62 2015
  658.4'02—dc23
                                                      2014044395

Henry Holt books are available for special promotions and premiums.
For details contact: Director, Special Markets.

First Edition 2015

Designed by Meryl Sussman Levavi

Printed in the United States of America

1   3   5   7   9   10   8   6   4   2

CONTENTS

FOREWORD

I met Brian Robertson when we shared the stage as presenters at a Conscious Capitalism conference in 2010 in California. When I heard his perspectives on a novel and dynamic way to structure and run an organization, I was enthralled.

At the time I was smarting from some of my own mistakes in this regard, and I was in the middle of a deep dive trying to figure out how to enable my small but eager company to run itself, without me having to play the CEO role. By that time, I knew I wasn't the best player for that play; I was more valuable to my organization as a spokesperson and as keeper of the flame of the GTD methodology popularized by my book *Getting Things Done*.

We had embarked on the path of attempting to scale our work to serve the growing interest around the world for its content. I knew I couldn't do it by myself, and that someone or something besides me would be required to lead that effort operationally. But entrusting the authority of "running the company" to a strong personality that might not totally be aligned with our critical DNA was tricky business. I sensed that what we were about as an organization was bigger than any of us individually. But putting someone "in charge" would mean handing over the reins of a simple but subtle and sophisticated IP that was trying to find its way in the world.

I wanted an organization that didn't need a CEO. At least not in the traditional sense.

Brian's message and the Holacracy model rocked my world—if it worked as he suggested it might, this was exactly what I was seeking. I rather quickly decided to go all in with our company and test it out. I needed to discover whether Holacracy worked, as soon as I could. The model seemed so powerful, I figured the only two options were to dismiss or adopt—either way, don't mess around.

I did (luckily) have an intuition that exploring Holacracy was going to be a five-year project. And even if Holacracy wasn't a good match for our organization's trajectory, the model made such cognitive sense that it would be worth the research—no matter that our fragile enterprise would be the crucible.

My career has revolved around productivity improvement—primarily for individuals, and subsequently for their organizations. I've known that when key individuals implement the best practices of Getting Things Done it can have significant ramifications for their whole ecosystem. But when I heard Brian speak about changing a fundamental operating process to achieve the organizational equivalent of "mind like water" (a metaphor I use for an individual's clarified state, achieved with GTD), I knew this was a frontier worth exploring.

As I write this, we are three-plus years into Holacracy implementation, and it seems my five-year projection may be accurate. To change the operating system of an organization is a daunting endeavor. We had prided ourselves on being a relatively with-it company—flexible, open, transparent . . . But as soon as we implemented some of the Holacracy processes, it became evident that some of our best-intentioned habits and practices would need to be transformed.

The fantastic part of the story is how much positive change occurred for us from the get-go. That positive change continues. Once you have tasted the increased clarity generated by the meeting and communication formats, it's hard to dismiss the system. Once you feel how much pressure is relieved when you let go of the necessity to have "heroic leaders," to reverse that direction would seem like being thrown back onto a very slippery slope.

As Brian indicates, Holacracy is not a panacea: it won't resolve all of an organization's tensions and dilemmas. But, in my experience, it does provide the most stable ground from which to recognize, frame, and address them.

There are times when many of us would love to prove Holacracy doesn't work. It's easy to blame the process as the perpetrator of our discomforts. But trying to poke a hole in the model is harder than implementing it! And in resolving the tensions that it has brought to the fore, it has also deepened our awareness of its practice and implications.

What's so wonderful is that the model doesn't care. As a matter of fact, getting rid of it is totally acceptable and allowed, within the model. But you'll want to use Holacracy to make that change as elegant as possible!

DAVID ALLEN
November 2014
Amsterdam, The Netherlands

PART ONE

EVOLUTION
AT WORK:
INTRODUCING
HOLACRACY

EVOLVING ORGANIZATION

If everyone had to think outside the box, maybe
it was the box that needed fixing.
—Malcolm Gladwell, *What the Dog Saw*

I learned my most important business lesson on the day I nearly
crashed an airplane. I was a student pilot working toward a
private pilot's license, and the day had come for my first long-
distance solo flight. I'd be flying alone to an airport far from
home, and with barely twenty hours of actual flight time under
my belt I was more than a little nervous. Hundreds of miles lay
ahead, and the only companionship I would have once airborne
was a well-worn bank of instruments in the cockpit of my little
two-seater airplane.

All seemed well just after takeoff, but before long I noticed
an unfamiliar light on the instrument panel. "Low Voltage," it
said. I wasn't sure what that meant—they don't teach new pilots
much about the plane's mechanics. I tapped the light, hoping
it was just a glitch, but nothing changed. Unsure how to respond,
I did what seemed natural at the time: I checked every other
instrument for anomalies. My airspeed and altitude were good.
The navigation aid told me I was perfectly on course. The fuel
gauge showed plenty of gas. All these instruments were telling

me I had nothing to worry about. So I accepted that consensus and effectively let the other instruments outvote the low-voltage light. I ignored it. It couldn't be too serious if nothing else was amiss, right?

This proved to be a very bad decision. It eventually left me completely lost, in a storm, with no lights and no radio, nearly out of gas, and violating controlled airspace near an international airport. And this near catastrophe started when I outvoted the low-voltage light, which, it turns out, was tuned in to different information than all the other instruments. Even though it was a minority voice, it was one I really needed to listen to at that moment. Dismissing its wisdom just because my other instruments didn't see any trouble was a shortsighted decision that could have cost me my life.

Fortunately I did make it down, shaken but unharmed. And in the months that followed, as I reflected on the decisions I had made that day, I came to an interesting conclusion. I was still making the same mistake—not in my plane, but in the team I was supposed to be leading at work. In fact, the near-fatal error I made in the cockpit is one made on a daily basis in most organizations.

An organization, like a plane, is equipped with sensors—not lights and gauges, but the human beings who energize its roles and sense reality on its behalf. Too often, an organization's "sensor" has critical information that is ignored and therefore goes unprocessed. One individual notices something important, but no one else sees it and no channels are available to process that insight into meaningful change. In this way, we often outvote the low-voltage lights of our organizations.

Our organizations become aware of whatever they need to respond to in their world through our human capacity to sense the reality around us. And we humans are all different—we have different talents, backgrounds, roles, fields of expertise, and so on—so we naturally sense different things. Where there are multiple people, there are multiple perspectives. Yet, on most teams, critical perspectives that aren't shared by the leader or by the majority are often ignored or dismissed. Even when we intend to do otherwise, we don't have a way to integrate differing perspectives, so we end up falling back in line with the leader or the majority. We outvote the person who may have key information we need to keep on course or move forward.

I've always been fascinated by *how we organize*—how we humans work together in pursuit of a purpose. Before I started my own business, I was often frustrated when I sensed something that wasn't working or that could be improved, only to find there wasn't much I could do with that awareness, at least not without heroic effort in the face of bureaucracy, politics, and long, painful meetings. I didn't just want to complain—I wanted to help. I wanted to process that *sense* I had into meaningful change. Yet I routinely encountered big obstacles to doing so. I learned early on that if the boss didn't share my frustration and I couldn't convince him relatively quickly, I might as well forget it. The information I was sensing was not going to have much impact. And if I was the low-voltage light, then the organization was in trouble.

The human capacity to *sense dissonance in the present moment and see the potential for change* strikes me as one of our most extraordinary gifts—our restless, never-satisfied, creative spirit that keeps us always reaching beyond where we are. When we feel that sense of frustration at a system that's not working, or a mistake that keeps getting repeated, or a process that seems inefficient and cumbersome, we are tuning in to a gap between how things *are* and how they *could be*. I call this a tension, because that's often how it is experienced, but I don't mean the word in a negative way. We might label this state a "problem" that "should" be fixed, or we might label it an "opportunity" to harness. Either way, that's just us projecting our meaning-making on the raw experience I'm calling a tension—*the perception of a specific gap between current reality and a sensed potential.*

We can hear an echo of that definition in the Latin root of the word *tendere*, which means "to stretch." As in a rubber band stretched between two points, there is tremendous energy held in these tensions we sense. That energy can be used to pull the organization toward each sensed potential—but only if we can effectively harness it. Yet of how many organizations can you genuinely say that any tension sensed by anyone, anywhere in the company, can be rapidly and reliably processed into meaningful change? As the cofounder of HP Dave Packard once said, "More companies die of indigestion than starvation."[1] Organizations sense and take in much more than they effectively process and digest. Consider the value that could be realized, instead, if our sensors had the capacity to dynamically update workflows, expectations, and even the very structure of the organization, in light of whatever tensions arise while getting the work done, without causing harm elsewhere in the process. That's a tall order, yet I've seen firsthand what can happen in an organization when its systems can do that, and the change goes well beyond creating better work environments or more effective processes. It can catalyze a much deeper transformation by unleashing the power of evolutionary design on the organization itself.

Evolution may not be a common topic within the business world, but its workings have an unparalleled capacity to produce exquisitely crafted systems that thrive amidst complexity. Said another way, evolution is the most intelligent designer around. As the economist Eric D. Beinhocker writes, "We are accustomed to thinking of evolution in a biological context, but modern evolutionary theory views evolution as something much more general. Evolution is an *algorithm*; it is an all-purpose formula for innovation . . . that, through its special brand of trial and error, creates new designs and solves difficult problems."[2] Markets, he explains, are highly dynamic, but the "brutal truth" is that the vast majority of companies are not. Organizations have very little capacity to evolve and adapt. They are subject to evolution's process at the market level and may survive or die as a result, but they are rarely adaptive organisms themselves, at least on more than a superficial level.

How can we make an organization not just *evolved* but *evolutionary*? How can we reshape a company into an evolutionary organism—one that can sense and adapt and learn and integrate? In Beinhocker's words, "The key to doing better is to 'bring evolution inside' and get the wheels of differentiation, selection, and amplification spinning *within* a company's four walls."[3] One powerful way to do that is to harness the tremendous sensing power of the human consciousness available to our organizations. Each tension human beings sense is a signpost telling us how the organization could evolve to better express its purpose. When those tensions can be processed quickly and effectively, at least to the extent that they relate to the organization's work, then the organization can benefit from an enhanced capacity to dynamically and continually evolve.

While this may be a compelling idea, it's one much easier expressed than put into practice. Our organizations today are simply not designed to rapidly evolve on the basis of inputs from many sensors. Most modern organizations are built on a basic blueprint that matured in the early 1900s and hasn't changed much since. This industrial-age paradigm operates on a principle I call "predict and control": they seek to achieve stability and success through up-front planning, centralized control, and preventing deviation. Rather than continually evolving an organization's design on the basis of real tensions sensed by real people, the predict-and-control approach focuses on designing the "perfect" system up front to prevent tensions (and then on reorganizing once those at the top realize they didn't quite get it right).

This model worked well enough in the relatively simple and static environments faced in the era in which it matured: the industrial age. In fact, it was a leap forward from previous approaches, enabling new levels of coordination, production, and progress. In today's postindustrial world, however, organizations face significant new challenges: increasing complexity, enhanced transparency, greater interconnection, shorter time horizons, economic and environmental instability, and demands to have a more positive impact on the world. Yet even when leaders embrace the need for new approaches, the predict-and-control foundation of the modern organization often fails to provide the agility desired and needed in this landscape of rapid change and dynamic complexity. And the structure of the modern organization rarely helps ignite the passion and creativity of the workforce. In short, today's organizations are quickly becoming obsolete.

As the wheels of change turn faster and faster in our increasingly chaotic global economy, it is becoming imperative that companies are able to adapt more quickly. As the management expert Gary Hamel recently said at the World Business Forum in New York, "The world is becoming more turbulent than organizations are becoming adaptable. Organizations were not built for these kinds of changes."[4]

I found this out the hard way in my early experience working in organizations. Most tensions sensed by individuals, including me, simply had nowhere to go. Tensions are just not recognized as among the organization's greatest resources. When I realized that my boss wasn't able to make use of my human capacity to sense and respond, I did the only logical thing: I became a boss myself. Now I could really process whatever it was I sensed, right? Well, there was still a higher boss to act as a bottleneck, and another, and another. After climbing the corporate ladder for a while, I realized that the only way I was going to have the freedom to respond to every tension I sensed would be to drop out of the system completely and start my own company.

So I did. And I loved it—for a while. But I soon discovered that even as the CEO of my own software company I was limited. The organizational structure and management system itself became a bottleneck for processing everything I sensed, and the sheer lack of hours in a day became a limiting factor: there was far too much complexity landing on my desk for the organization to fully harness even my own consciousness as its CEO. And that wasn't the worst of it.

The more painful realization was that I had built just the kind of system I had worked for so long to get out of. Everyone who worked for me was in the same position I had been in. And my organization was not much more able to harness their capacity to sense reality than any other. I tried to be the best leader I could—to empower people and be sensitive to their needs and issues, to develop myself, to be a more conscious "servant leader"—yet despite my best efforts, I kept running into an invisible barrier. The underlying structure, systems, and culture of a modern corporation do not allow for the rapid processing and responsiveness necessary to fully harness the power of every human sensor, no matter what I did as a leader. So I began searching for a better way.

An Operating System Upgrade

I'm certainly not the first to point out the limits of a traditional organizational design and the need for new approaches. Over the past couple of decades, ever more books, articles, and talks have shared perspectives on organization that are clearly beyond our conventional norms. While each of these authors and pioneers has his or her unique focus, it's hard not to notice some general emphases—on more adaptability, more flexible structures, a broader stakeholder orientation; on working with uncertainty; on new ways of engaging the workforce; on more systemic approaches to business, and so on. Each of these perspectives offers a glimpse of what may be a cohesive new paradigm taking shape at the edge of organizational practice today.

Yet despite the power of these new-paradigm ideas and techniques, I routinely see a huge obstacle to their deployment: when they're applied in an organizational system that's still conventionally structured, there's a major paradigm clash. At best, the novel techniques become a "bolt-on"—something that affects just one aspect of the organization and remains in continual conflict with the other systems around it. A great new meeting technique helps empower a team, for instance, but those team members are still constrained by a power structure at play outside of the meeting and throughout the rest of the company. At worst, the "corporate antibodies" come out and reject the bolted-on technique, a foreign entity that doesn't quite fit the predominant mental model of how an organization should be structured and run. In either case, the novel practice fails to realize its full potential, however promising, and we don't get much of a paradigm shift in the organizational system.

This is a major challenge for anyone applying leading-edge ideas and techniques in conventional systems. How can we evolve some aspect of how we organize, when the innovations we try to use clash with the older paradigm still at play? Everything I've experienced continually points back to this conclusion: to really transform an organization, we must move beyond bolting on changes and instead focus on upgrading the most foundational aspects of the way the organization functions. For example, consider the way power and authority are formally defined and exercised, the way the organization is structured, and the way we establish who can expect what, and from whom—or who can make which decisions, and within what limits. When we change things at this level, we are effectively installing a new organizational operating system, infusing new capacities into the core of how the organization functions, so that we can move beyond applying changes to a system that's fundamentally at odds with the very process of change itself.

If you're old enough to remember the days when most PCs ran MS-DOS, consider the leap in capabilities that came with a new operating system like Windows, or the shift from the old Apple II to the Macintosh. It would have been hard to imagine, back in the eighties, that my black screen with blocky green text would soon be replaced by an interactive, self-updating, user-friendly graphical interface constantly connected to a worldwide virtual network, with instant access to the world's collective store of information—and that all this would be available on a device that fits in my pocket.

Despite the radical difference a good operating system makes, we can easily ignore it and take it for granted—it's just an underlying platform, often invisible, though it shapes everything that's built on top of it. Your computer's operating system defines the space in which everything else happens and the core rules by which everything else must play. It defines how the overall system is structured, how different processes interact and cooperate, how power is distributed and allocated between applications, and so on.

Likewise, the operating system underpinning an organization is easy to ignore, yet it's the foundation on which we build our business processes (the "apps" of organization), and it shapes the human culture as well. Perhaps because of its invisibility, we haven't seen many robust alternatives or significant improvements to our modern top-down, predict-and-control, "CEO is in charge" OS. When we unconsciously accept that as our only choice, the best we can do is counteract some of its fundamental weaknesses by bolting on new processes or trying to improve organization-wide culture. But just as many of our current software applications wouldn't run well on MS-DOS, the new processes, techniques, or cultural changes we might try to adopt simply won't run well on an operating system built around an older paradigm.

While I didn't realize it at the start of my journey, my personal quest to find better ways to work together would eventually lead me to focus on the fundamental "social technology" of how we organize. After many years of experimentation, across several organizations, a comprehensive new operating system emerged, through my efforts and those of many others. Eventually, we called it Holacracy (a term whose origins I'll explain in more detail later in this book). What is Holacracy? Essentially, it's a new social technology for governing and operating an organization, defined by a set of core rules distinctly different from those of a conventionally governed organization. Holacracy includes the following elements:

- a constitution, which sets out the "rules of the game" and redistributes authority
- a new way to structure an organization and define people's roles and spheres of authority within it
- a unique decision-making process for updating those roles and authorities
- a meeting process for keeping teams in sync and getting work done together

As of this writing, Holacracy is powering hundreds of organizations of many types and sizes around the world, including

HolacracyOne, the organization where I work day to day (so we eat our own dog food, as they say).

In the chapters that follow, I'll unpack how Holacracy distributes authority, and how this translates into a new organizational structure. Then, in Part II, I'll walk you through the nuts and bolts of how the operating system works—its structures, processes, and systems. These chapters are not designed as a how-to guide for installing Holacracy in your company; think of them more as an experiential workshop where you can participate in various scenarios and simulations and get a taste of what it's like to work in a Holacracy-powered organization. Finally, in Part III, I'll offer some advice and guidelines for how you might go about implementing what you've learned in this book, and what to expect when you do.

I'll continually attempt to convey how Holacracy looks and feels in practice, by sharing stories and experiences frequently reported by those working in Holacracy-powered organizations. This is my attempt to address a core challenge of writing this book: Holacracy is above all a practice, not a theory, idea, or philosophy, and it is difficult to truly understand a practice without experiencing it. The practice of Holacracy itself came into being through practice—through trial and error, evolutionary adaptation, and ongoing experimentation, all in an effort simply to unleash more creative capacity for an organization to express its purpose. Because Holacracy wasn't created by sitting down and designing a system on the basis of certain ideas or principles, the challenge of conveying it through words and concepts becomes even more difficult. When I look back at the end result, I see that while I may have extracted certain principles, these were after-the-fact tools for understanding what had organically emerged from experimentation.

Therefore, I hope my readers will approach this book not as a set of ideas, principles, or philosophies, but as a guide to a new practice, which you may choose to use if it works for you and your business better than whatever you are currently doing. This is where Holacracy really comes alive—in the day-to-day work of processing tensions into meaningful change, for the sake of whatever purpose the organization is here to express. It is thus my goal in this book to convey at least a glimpse of the *experience* of practicing Holacracy, and give you a taste of what an evolution-powered organization makes possible.

DISTRIBUTING AUTHORITY

A good constitution is infinitely better than the best despot.

—THOMAS BABINGTON MACAULAY, *Milton*

"Research shows that every time the size of a city doubles, innovation or productivity per resident increases by 15 percent. But when companies get bigger, innovation or productivity per employee generally goes down."

This fascinating piece of data was presented to me by a man with close-cropped dark hair, who cornered me soon after I finished a presentation at a business conference a couple of years ago. Many in the crowd wore business attire; he was dressed in jeans and a T-shirt, yet his air of quiet intensity belied his casual appearance.

"So," he continued, "I'm interested in how we can create organizations that are more like cities and less like bureaucratic corporations."

The unknown gentleman peppered me with questions for the next ten minutes or so. "Do you think Holacracy could achieve this?" Yes, I replied. "What's the biggest company you've ever worked with? How many companies are using it?" I did my best to answer the man's questions, with one eye on the clock, knowing I was late for the next session. As I hurried down the hallway, I realized I had never even asked his name, or why he was so passionately interested in this topic.

Later that day, when I took my seat for the evening's keynote speech, I was surprised to see the man I'd been talking to earlier step out on stage, to enthusiastic applause. My interrogator was Tony Hsieh, the unassuming CEO of the online retailer Zappos, author of *Delivering Happiness*, and one of the most visionary and innovative leaders in business today.

Tony and I were able to continue our conversation later during the conference, and he shared more of what he was trying to achieve. "Zappos is growing," he told me. "We've reached fifteen hundred employees, and we need to scale without losing our entrepreneurial culture or getting bogged down in bureaucracy. So I'm trying to find a way to run Zappos more like a city."

"Yes!" I replied, happy to find someone who shared my interest in this kind of challenge. We spoke about the difference between the bureaucratic organization of a company and the self-organization of people in a city. In an urban environment, people share space and resources locally, understanding territorial boundaries and responsibilities. Of course, there are laws and governing bodies to define and enforce those laws, but people don't have bosses ordering them around all the time. If the residents of our cities had to wait for authorization from the boss for every decision they made, the city would quickly grind to a halt. Yet in our companies we see a very different organizing principle at play.

How Do You Distribute Authority?

Hsieh's analogy points to the critical question I had faced as I worked to create a new, more agile and responsive organizational operating system: how do you enable an organization to effectively self-organize?

Another of my favorite metaphors for what I'm looking to achieve in an organization is a system we are all very familiar with: the human body. The rather miraculous human body functions efficiently and effectively not with a top-down command system but with a distributed system—a network of autonomous self-organizing entities distributed throughout the body. Each of these entities, which are your cells, organs, and organ systems, has capacity to take in messages, process them, and generate output. Each has a function and has the autonomy to organize how it completes that function.

Think about the amount of information your body processes from moment to moment. It's extraordinary. Is there any way that the body could function if it centralized all information processing at the top, in the conscious mind? Imagine, for example, if your white blood cells, when sensing a disease, had to send the information to your conscious mind and wait for you to sign off on the production of antibodies. Or if your adrenal glands, sensing that you are reacting to danger, had to wait for your orders before producing adrenaline to give you the energy for fight or flight? This wouldn't work well at all. And yet it's how we expect our organizations to function.

The more forward-thinking leaders in contemporary corporate culture are all too aware of the problems with the top-down, predict-and-control paradigm. They see its limitations and feel its unhealthy consequences. But what is the noble, well-intentioned leader to do? Often, they attempt to empower others, like good parents seeking to empower their children. There's a predominant view today that improving organizations means getting highly developed, wise, conscious leaders in power to serve as "good parents."

The problem with this approach was articulated most clearly

for me in a play I went to see several years ago, written by one of my favorite business writers, Barry Oshry. It was a brilliant drama about organizations, with one scene that really struck me. A much-loved leader had just been fired, and one of his team, lamenting the departure of his boss, turned to his coworker and asked: "Who will empower us now?"

I found the intentional irony in the statement both poignant and illuminating. Of course, it is a fundamentally disempowered victim's stance to need someone else to empower you. And it pointed to the unfortunate side effect of that leader's well-intentioned work: in heroically "empowering others" within an inherently disempowering corporate structure, he paradoxically put others in the role of victims.

No matter how much today's best leaders may want to empower others and give them a voice, the formal power structure in most modern corporations is that of a dictatorship. As one of our clients put it, "From the beginning, my cofounder and I wanted to run our company in an egalitarian way, so that we were all in it together. But the way our company was structured, and the way the process was set up, we were still trying to 'run' the company, based on an org chart, with people reporting to me. We didn't have a process to approach it any other way—not one that we could trust to make the system function."

This ultimate reliance on the CEO or equivalent limits the capacity to harness all tensions sensed throughout an organization, and creates a potential single point of failure in the organization's capacity to effectively govern itself. As the business writer Gary Hamel puts it, "Give someone monarch-like authority, and sooner or later there will be a royal screw-up." Hamel further points out that in most cases, "the most powerful managers are the ones furthest from frontline realities. All too often, decisions made on an Olympian peak prove to be unworkable on the ground."[5]

A friend told me a story that illustrates this point, about a factory that had recently hired a new CEO. Eager to set an example, the new leader went down to the shop floor one day. He saw a group of workers busy at their stations, while one guy was just leaning against the wall, watching. The CEO marched up to this guy and asked: "You, how much money do you make?" "Two or three hundred bucks a week," the man answered, looking a little taken aback. The CEO pulled out his wallet, and handed him $600. "Here's two weeks' pay—you're fired." As the man quickly left the building, the CEO turned to the shop floor and declared, "That's not what we do around here. We keep busy!" As he was heading back to his office, he stopped to ask one of the stunned workers what that guy actually did in the company. The response: "That was the pizza delivery guy."

This is a humorous example, but too often the results of autocratic power are anything but funny when that power is wielded within another's domain. It creates tensions that have no way of being effectively processed.

What are we to do if we want to move beyond an autocratic management model and the need for empowerment within a disempowering system? How can we reap the benefits of true autonomy, as we do in a city or in our own bodies, while also meeting genuine needs for organizational alignment and control? Some companies boldly abandon convention and attempt to skip an explicit power structure altogether, or use only a minimally defined one. That can work to a point, but it presents an insidious danger: if no explicit power structure is in place, an implicit structure will emerge. Decisions need to be made and expectations set, one way or another, and social norms will develop around how those functions are carried out. Organizations that attempt to forgo an explicit power structure thus end up with an implicit one, which is often quite political and

somewhat resistant to change. This less-than-conscious structure may still be more effective than a conventional management hierarchy in some contexts, but I think we can do a lot
better.

Some small start-ups and nonprofits try running their organizations via consensus. I tried this in the early days at my
start-up software company. I was looking for an approach that
allowed every voice to be heard, so it seemed logical to give
everyone a say in decision making. The reality, however, was
that not many decisions were made at all, and we spent all our
time in meetings rather than getting work done. There is a big
difference, I discovered, between having a voice and being able
to *do* something with your voice—being able to actually process what you sense into meaningful change. Consensus didn't
accomplish that. In fact, all it resulted in was long painful
meetings where we would try to force everyone to see things
the same way. That isn't helpful or healthy, and it only gets
worse as an organization grows.

So consensus doesn't scale well at all, and such impractical quantities of time and energy are required to reach a decision that the system gets bypassed more often than not. This
leaves consensus-based organizations with the same problems
as those organizations with no explicit structure. Even when
consensus is achieved, the result is often a watered-down group
decision that becomes very difficult to change, saddling
would-be innovators with less-than-ideal entrenched structures
to navigate. While consensus-based approaches are often moti-
vated by a genuine desire to embrace and honor more people's
voices, they are rarely effective at harnessing true self-
organization and agility throughout an enterprise.

If an organization wants to be dynamic and responsive, then
to reject autocratic authority entirely just won't work. In fact,

individuals need to be given the power to respond to issues "locally," within their domain or work, without having to get everyone else's buy-in or rely on an empowering leader for permission. To move beyond the limits of empowerment and the tyranny of consensus, we need a *system* that empowers everyone.

Which brings us back to Hsieh's metaphor of the city—and, in fact, modern civil society as a whole. As a citizen, you don't require a benevolent dictator to "empower" you to act autonomously; rather, the societal framework around you is designed to prevent others from claiming power over you to begin with. This is the shift at the heart of Holacracy: the recognition that when the core authority structure and processes of an organization fundamentally hold space for everyone to have and use power, and do not allow anyone—even a leader—to co-opt the power of others, then we no longer need to rely on leaders who empower others. Instead we have something much more powerful: a space where we can all find our own empowerment, and a system that protects that space regardless of the actions of any one individual, whatever his or her position.

Power to the Process

With Holacracy, distributing authority is not just a matter of taking power out of the hands of a leader and giving it to someone else or even to a group. Rather, the seat of power shifts from the person at the top to a *process*, which is defined in detail in a written constitution. Holacracy's constitution is a generic document applicable to any organization wishing to use the method; once formally adopted, the Holacracy constitution acts as the core rulebook for the organization. Its rules and processes reign supreme, and trump even the person who adopted it. Like a constitutionally backed congress defining laws that even a president can't ignore, so too does the Holacracy constitution define the seat of authority for the organization as resting in a legislative process, not an autocratic ruler.

You can find the Holacracy constitution online at holacracy .org/constitution, but you don't need to read it to learn Holacracy. Reading a rulebook is rarely the best approach to learning a complex new game. It usually works better to simply learn the basic guidelines and then start playing, turning to the rulebook as a reference when needed. Still, it's critical to know that there *is* a rulebook, and to agree to abide by it; a game isn't a game when one person gets to make up the rules as they go. When I work with an organization on the path of implementing Holacracy, the very first step is for the CEO to formally adopt the Holacracy constitution and cede his or her power into its rule system. By heroically releasing authority into the system's embrace, the leader paves the way for an authentic distribution of power through every level of the organization.

This shift from personal leadership to constitutionally derived power is essential to Holacracy's new paradigm. Even with the best of intentions and great leaders, a top-down authority system leads almost inevitably to a parent-child dynamic between the boss and the employee. Familiar archetypes are almost impossible to avoid; the result is that workers feel disempowered and victimized, and managers feel overwhelmed by the sense that it is up to them to take on all the responsibility and deal with everyone's tensions. Holacracy tells managers, "It's no longer your job to solve everyone's problems and take on responsibility for everything." And it tells workers, "You have the responsibility, *and the authority,* to deal with your own tensions." This simple shift lifts everyone involved out of the parent-child dynamic that is so deeply ingrained in our organizational culture, and into a functional relationship between autonomous, self-managing adults, each of whom has the power to "lead" his or her role in service of the organization's purpose.

When this shift happens in the companies I've worked with, it comes as a revelation and a challenge for everyone involved. The workers realize that they are no longer just employees following orders. They have real power and authority—and with those comes responsibility. They no longer have a parentlike manager to solve their problems. The managers, on the other hand, often feel liberated from the burden of management, but have to find a new sense of their own value and contribution, and shift how they're accustomed to using and holding authority. One of the more interesting parts of my job is to remind CEOs who have recently adopted Holacracy, "You no longer have the authority to make that decision." And, on the flip side, I also have to remind others that "you have the accountability and authority to make that decision; it's yours to own, and it's not the boss's job to tell you what to do or bless your decision."

Interestingly, most CEOs I've worked with find this shift to be a tremendous relief. This may be surprising to some. Bernard Marie Chiquet, a Holacracy coach based in Paris and a past CEO himself, says that people often think it must be difficult to convince CEOs to give up their power, yet that's not his experience at all. He's found that many seasoned CEOs like the idea of releasing their personally held power into an organizational process, if they can find a safe way to do so that more effectively meets the organization's needs. I've found the same to be true. Over a meal we shared, Evan Williams, the cofounder of Twitter and, more recently, of Medium, described the dread he felt when, after leaving Twitter, he considered building another company in a traditional CEO role, with all its burdens and distractions from the creative work he most enjoyed. He adopted Holacracy at Medium partly so that burden wouldn't rest solely on his shoulders; far from needing "convincing," he was drawn to Holacracy specifically because of its distribution of authority.

This is also what intrigued Zappos' Hsieh about Holacracy: its promise of a safe and practical way to distribute real power and therefore allow for self-organization, through a constitutionally defined governance process. After our initial encounter, Hsieh invited me to meet his team and decided to pilot Holacracy in a small department within his organization. The pilot was successful enough that in 2013 he went on to roll out Holacracy throughout his company. I was thrilled—and just a little apprehensive. This would be by far our biggest adoption yet. How would Holacracy work at the scale of a fifteen-hundred-employee company? Would it create the self-organizing, citylike collaborative environment that Hsieh was looking for? I knew it had the potential to do exactly that in smaller organizations, so I was eager to see it play out on this bigger stage.

What the team at Zappos experienced over the next year, as had many smaller companies before them, is that Holacracy can genuinely empower everyone. "The power that managers had is now distributed to every single employee," said Alexis Gonzales-Black, who worked on the team that spearheaded the rollout. "Everyone's now responsible for taking their experiences in their job to drive the company forward." Making the shift wasn't easy—"It's training managers to step back and people to step forward that's really difficult," Gonzales-Black notes. "With Holacracy in place, each individual can step up to solve his own tension, process it openly and freely. But it's not a skill that naturally comes to people. The more you practice Holacracy the better you become at it; you need to build and train that muscle." As people became accustomed to their new authority, what she noticed was a start-up mentality in which everyone is encouraged to ask, "If this was my company, what would I do?"[6]

By distributing power in this way, Holacracy liberates those within the organization to be simultaneously more autonomous and more collaborative. In a Holacracy-powered organization, there are no more managers—which, as one of my clients recently put it, "sounds like democratic chaos, but the truth is it's quite autocratic." With authority clear and distributed, no one has to tiptoe around an issue to build buy-in, or push to get others to see things the same way they do. This frees people to take action confidently, knowing that a legislative process has granted them that authority with due input and consideration. And at the time same, someone with clear autonomy is free to ask for help, input, and dialogue, and others are free to give it and pitch their opinions, without any risk of the process devolving to a consensus deadlock or an autocratic decree from a busy leader too far removed from the issue. As soon as the authority holder gets enough input to confidently make a decision, he or she can comfortably cut off the dialogue, thank those involved, and make that decision. And all of this builds greater flexibility, responsiveness, and adaptability into the organization.

It also liberates the creative energy of former managers in surprising and powerful ways. To return to our earlier analogy, if the human body weren't a distributed-authority system, with the various cells, organs, and systems each holding clear autonomy, authority, and responsibility, the conscious mind would have a huge management burden. But because our conscious energy is not needed for the moment-to-moment decision making of our physical functioning, it is freed up to engage with all the extraordinary creative endeavors that define human culture. I think that's true in organizations as well. When you get all parts of the organization locally owning and managing real responsibility, responding autonomously and effectively, it frees the former "bosses" to focus on a totally different level—to engage with the bigger creative questions of how to express the organization's purpose in the world.

Introducing Governance

There's a technical term for the process by which we assign power or authority in an organization: "governance." In most organizations running without Holacracy, there may be some explicit governance performed at the very top or set out in the bylaws, but otherwise little conscious attention is given to defining clear authorities and responsibilities. And when attention *is* given, the context is often a big reorganization that creates as many problems as it resolves and that ends up detached from the real needs of getting work done. With Holacracy in place, governance happens consciously and regularly, distributed throughout the organization. It is no longer the function of any single leader, but becomes an ongoing process that happens on a team-by-team level in special "governance meetings."

Holacracy thus takes some of the organizational design functions that traditionally reside with a CEO or executive team and places them into *processes* that are enacted throughout the organization, with everyone's participation. This governance process distributes authority and clarifies expectations throughout an organization, and is driven by those doing its work and sensing tensions along the way. In governance, tensions are harnessed to clarify not only questions such as, "Who makes which decisions and within what limits?," but also the expectations others can hold of them while they use that authority. Governance generates organizational clarity, then continually evolves it to integrate the team's latest learnings and fit its changing realities.

How It Works

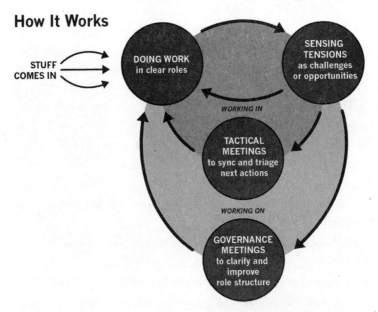

It's easiest to understand governance in relation to the other sphere of organizational life, which we're generally more used to: "operations." Operations is about getting work done—identifying outcomes to achieve, making specific decisions, allocating resources, taking actions, and coordinating those actions with others. Governance is about *how* we work—the pattern of how we organize, as distinct from the specific decisions we make within that pattern. It is a meta-level approach to the business. Governance is about the structure of the organization's work, and the authorities and expectations that go along with it. Both governance and operations may be informed by a relevant strategy, meaning a guiding theme or rule of thumb to apply as a team navigates in its journey to express the organization's purpose.

A simple example from my company can illustrate the difference between these spheres of activity. We deliver public Holacracy trainings, among other services, and of course we need to pick a hotel to serve as the venue. Each possibility will have its own benefits and drawbacks. The choice is an example of an operational question and decision. The governance question, however, would be "What role has the authority to make that decision, within what constraints, and what can we expect from that role as a condition of its having this authority?" Whoever fills that role will use that authority, granted in governance, to make the specific operational decision of which hotel to use for any given training. The person may also apply a broader strategy as a general guideline to help make that decision—a topic we'll return to later in this book.

Almost anyone involved in an organization has engaged in operations and making decisions, and probably has applied some kind of strategy to guide his or her decisions. However, it is quite a shift for most people to engage with governance, because most organizations have little in the way of an explicit governance process or of the clarity that such a process produces; what governance does exist is often irrelevant and ignored (for instance, the typical "job description"), with no clear process for dynamically updating it. Yet governance clarity that maintains its relevance is deeply powerful. It answers questions such as:

What are the ongoing activities we need to pay attention to, and who will own each?

What expectations can I reasonably hold of others, and vice versa?

Who will make which decisions, and within what limits?

What decisions can I make and what actions can I take without having to call a meeting?

What policies or constraints will we honor in our work together?

How can we change the answers to these questions as we learn better ways of working together?

When any group of people comes together to accomplish a specific task or mission, such questions come up. Even if we don't discuss them, we make assumptions about the answers. Just watch a group of children playing a game: implicit governance defines the rules, roles, and parameters within which they play. In many situations, implicit governance works just fine—until, for some reason, it doesn't work anymore. Perhaps implicit assumptions conflict, or perhaps someone wants to evolve the historically operating norm to integrate some new learning. Whenever there's a need to align or evolve implicit norms and assumptions, an explicit governance process can be transformative.

Yet most organizations today have no such explicit process, at least beyond a board level. Instead, most organizational bylaws (or their equivalent) formally vest the power of governing the organization's operations in some leader at the top—a CEO, managing director, or whatever label is used. This CEO may then define authorities and expectations for the whole company, or delegate some of the power to do so, although rarely is this definition or delegation done either with any significant clarity or fast enough to keep pace with all the available learning opportunities. In a world that is changing faster every day, governance needs to become an ongoing part of how an organization operates, and questions of governance are just as relevant on the shop floor as they are in the boardroom. What's more, the people working on the front lines are often better positioned to drive continual improvements within their context and monitor the results from day to day. To return to our earlier example, the floor manager is unlikely to fire the pizza guy. But without an explicit governance process for each team, opportunities to improve organizational patterns will remain largely centralized: they'll stay with the leader who holds the power to autocratically dictate the organization's structure—the person at the top.

When we effectively distribute power to those on the front lines, we dramatically enhance an organization's capacity to harness input and capture learning—thus solving a problem many leaders struggle with as their companies grow. Evan Williams put it this way: "In the past, I've hired these amazing people, but I felt like I was getting less and less of them as the company got bigger. Part of that was because they had ideas or concerns or perspectives that were relevant outside their particular area, but it wasn't clear what to do with those."[7] All too often, this inability to engage leaves workers vulnerable and disconnected, with no healthy or useful outlet for improving the status quo. Williams described how Holacracy "allows you to really take advantage of everybody's perspectives and ideas, and even if you don't accept them all, at least it lowers their anxiety because there's a route to process them, and there's transparency."

While those lower down the corporate ladder in conventional organizations may find that Holacracy relieves the frustration of not being heard, those at the top, who are often equally frustrated, can find it a tremendous relief as well. Leaders face overwhelming complexity and overload, with more challenges and information than they can effectively process. David Allen, the creator of the Getting Things Done system, is one of the world's foremost experts on personal organization and productivity, yet even he admits that the expectations placed on him as a conventional CEO were unmanageable. "As the person sitting up at the top," he told me, "I barely had the bandwidth to make a small portion of the decisions floating up to me. So either I wasn't available to make those decisions, or I couldn't do so responsibly."[8] By distributing the job of evolving the organization across the entire company, Holacracy decreases the overload at the top and the disengagement found elsewhere, while instilling new capacities for learning and adaptability throughout the organization. David went on to describe the results of adopting Holacracy in his company as "a huge relief. This paradigm shift has taken a huge burden off me psychologically and even physically."

Michael Gerber, the author of the classic entrepreneurship manual *The E-Myth*, points out that one of the biggest mistakes entrepreneurs tend to make is that they get stuck working *in* their businesses rather than working *on* their businesses.[9] Working *on* the business is the essence of governance, and the Holacracy constitution makes the process explicit at every level of the organization and for everyone involved. The results of this governance process then enable people to work *in* the business—to conduct its operations—with greater autonomy and speed. It's a lot easier and safer to execute quickly and autonomously and get the work done when you know exactly what authority you have, what's expected of you, and what limits you need to honor, and when you have a process to update this knowledge as learning happens or the environment changes.

Discovering Purpose

I have repeatedly mentioned the concept of an organization's "purpose." While that's not so unusual in a book about business nowadays, it's worth taking a moment to explain what I mean by "purpose," and what I don't. Sometimes, when I am working with a group of founders, partners, or board members, particularly for very human-focused organizations, I will ask each person to share his or her deepest hopes, dreams, ambitions, and desires for the organization. It's always a powerful moment, filled with authenticity and inspiration, as those present share what they most want to see the organization do and be in the world. And then I'll say, "Let me point out the biggest obstacle to uncovering the purpose of this organization. It's everything you just said—your hopes, desires, and so on."

People are usually taken aback by this statement, but once they get the point, it can be quite a revelation. Of course there's nothing wrong with their own hopes, dreams, ambitions, and desires, yet these things are often projected onto the organization and obscure *its* purpose. To return to the metaphor I was using earlier in the chapter, they risk treating the organization the way an overbearing parent might treat a child. Most of the parents I work with understand that projecting their own hopes and dreams onto their children will inhibit those children from finding their own paths in life. Societally, we have come to accept that children are not property to be shaped to their parents' wills; they are independent beings with unique skills, talents, and passions. When we attempt to force our visions upon them, we resist this reality—often to the detriment of both parties, and definitely to the detriment of the relationship. I find the same is true of our organizations and their relationship with founders, leaders, and other stewards.

Every organization has some potential or creative capacity it is best suited to sustainably express in the world, given everything available to it—its history, workforce, resources, founders, brand, capital, relationships . . . That's what I mean by its purpose or raison d'être—its reason for being. This isn't necessarily the purpose that we founders or leaders want for the organization, although it's typically seeded by the founders—in a company's formative years, "everything available to it" may be little more than the founders' passions, and those will shape the purpose, at least for a while. When parents let go of their own personal dreams for their children, they create space to find out what those children were really born to do—what creative impulse is waiting to express itself through each child. In the same way, when we let go of the idea that "I want my company to do X," we can find the organization's own creative impulse—the deepest potential or creative capacity it can sustainably express in the world, given everything available to it. Said another way, what does this organization want to be in the world, and what does the world need this organization to be?

This isn't to say that every organization will have a beautiful, creative, visionary purpose. Some expressions of purpose that are mundane indeed are nevertheless authentic to the organization. The purpose of a garbage disposal company might be simply "to create cleaner cities"—which may not be glamorous, but nonetheless gets at the "why" behind what the company does, and expresses a potential that the company is well suited to bring about in the world. At HolacracyOne, we have captured our best understanding of our organization's purpose in two words: "Exquisite Organization."

Getting there was a process of discovery: we did not decide on this purpose, we discovered it. I say "discovered" rather than "decided" because getting clear on purpose is more like detective work than like creative work. What you are looking for is already there, waiting to be found—it is no more a decision than your child's purpose is. Simply ask yourself: "On the basis of our current context and the resources, talents, and capacities at our disposal, the products or services we offer, the history of the company and its market space, and so on, what's the deepest potential it can help create or manifest in the world? Why does the world need it?"

Don't worry if you can't immediately come up with a succinct phrase capturing your organization's purpose. Like everything in Holacracy, uncovering purpose is a dynamic and continuing process, and the practical applicability of your purpose is much more important than the elegance of its wording. The purpose isn't something you frame and put on the wall to inspire you; it's a tool you use daily as you go about your business. As you shift into a distributed-authority model, purpose becomes the anchor for decision making at every level and in every sphere of activity. Governance is about how we structure the organization and its roles to best express that purpose, and operations is about using that structure to bring about that purpose in the world. The whole point of Holacracy is to allow an organization to better express its purpose. In this way and many others, Holacracy is not a governance process "of the people, by the people, for the people"—it's governance *of* the organization, *through* the people, *for* the purpose.

ORGANIZATIONAL STRUCTURE

Everything is vague to a degree you do not realize
till you have tried to make it precise.

—BERTRAND RUSSELL, *The Philosophy
of Logical Atomism*

If we want to distribute authority and embed evolutionary capacities in the way we do business, we need a way to structure our organizations that is conducive to that process. The traditional pyramid-shaped management hierarchy is one structural option, but it's often far less than ideal for enabling distributed authority and evolutionary design. Holacracy offers an alternative way to structure an organization. But before we get down to redesigning the org chart, let's take a moment to discuss what "structure" means in an organization.

I find a simple distinction used by the organizational theorist Elliott Jaques particularly helpful and clarifying. He identified three distinct types or meanings of "structure" that can be useful in any organization. First, there is the "formal structure"—the org chart and the job descriptions. I'm sure you know what these look like, but how often do you actually use them? How many times during a typical day at work do you go and look at job descriptions to get clarity on what you need to focus on and what you can expect from others? When I ask this question, most people tend to laugh. Many confess that they wouldn't even know where to find their organization's job descriptions. The formal structure in most organizations is far removed from real day-to-day events and needs, so that job descriptions are little more than formalized bureaucratic artifacts. In many cases, they are out-of-date and irrelevant by the time they roll off the printer.

CORPORATE STRUCTURE
HOW WE BELIEVE IT TO BE

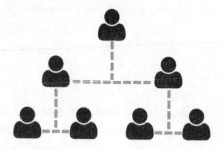

When the organization's formal structure offers little practical guidance, we humans, as the creative beings we are, work around it to get the job done. This gives rise to what Jaques calls the "extant structure." This is the structure that is actually operating—the often implicit reality of who's making what decisions or who owns which projects. An organization's extant structure is usually shaped by personal relationships and politics. As we work together in this way, cultural norms develop, and we start aligning with them, creating an implicit structure that becomes the unconscious "way things are done." Jaques goes on to point out a third potential structure: the "requisite structure," which is the structure that would be most natural and best suited to the work and purpose of the organization—the structure that "wants to be."

CORPORATE STRUCTURE
HOW IT REALLY WORKS

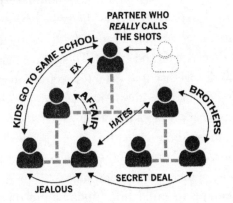

Earlier, in discussing the idea of sensing and processing tensions, we defined a tension as a gap between what is and what could be—a sensed potential that would somehow be more ideal. Using Jaques's language, we could say we're sensing a gap between the extant structure (what is) and the requisite structure (what could be). When we take that tension to a Holacracy governance meeting and process it into meaningful change, we end up evolving the formal structure to be more requisite—we refine the explicitly captured details of who does what and the authorities and expectations at play, so that they reflect a more ideal state. For example, if you were responsible for managing a production schedule, but kept feeling a tension because someone else in the organization was stepping on your toes and doubling up on tasks you'd already done, you could use the governance process to clarify that division of labor more effectively. So while we do have a formally captured structure in Holacracy, it is continually being refined and modified in response to tensions sensed by individuals as they go about their daily work, to reflect our best understanding of how we need to organize to most effectively get the work done.

Consequently, in a Holacracy-powered organization, people do refer to their own and others' job descriptions regularly, sometimes on a daily basis—because job descriptions contain relevant, accurate, clear, and useful information about what it makes sense to do and expect. This means that the way we actually work together (the extant structure) more closely reflects what's documented (the formal structure), which more closely reflects what's best for the organization (the requisite structure). Thus, these three structures become one and the same—at least for a time, until another tension is sensed, and this evolutionary process must continue.

Keeping in mind this fundamental distinction—that in Holacracy, "structure" is not fixed or solid, but continually evolving—let's look at the type of structure used in Holacracy and the various elements that make it up.

Nature's Structure

The type of structure used for organizations in Holacracy is not a traditional hierarchy, but a "holarchy." Arthur Koestler coined the term in his 1967 book *The Ghost in the Machine*. He defined a "holon" as "a whole that is a part of a larger whole" and a "holarchy" as "the connection between holons." Those may be strange and unfamiliar terms, but they describe something very familiar. Your own body is an example of a holarchy. Each cell in your body is a holon—both a self-contained, whole entity *and* a part of a larger whole, an organ. In the same way, each organ is itself a self-contained whole yet also a part of a larger whole—your body. That series of nested holons—cell to organ to organism—is an example of a holarchy.

We see this kind of structure all around us in the way nature organizes itself. Think about how particles interact to create atoms, which bond together into molecules, which group into crystals or proteins, for example—each being both a part and a whole. These holarchies simultaneously honor autonomy and enable self-organization at every level within. This is the kind of structure that Holacracy uses, and it's the root of the term itself: Holacracy means governance (-*cracy*) of and by the organizational holarchy (*hola-*).

When we consider a company through this lens of holons and holarchies, we might assume human beings were the smaller holons in the organizational system, embraced by larger holons of teams, departments, and so on. But human beings are not fully contained "parts of a company" the way cells are parts of an organ. Rather, we are separate autonomous entities who choose to show up and "energize" an organization's functions, organized in various "roles." Those roles *are* parts of the company, and are the most basic building block of Holacracy's structure. When we distribute authority, as discussed in the previous chapter, we distribute it not to individual humans, but to the roles that they fill. Particular roles are invested with the authority to carry out certain tasks and pursue particular aims. When the responsibilities attached to a role become too much for one individual to carry, that role may further need to break itself down into multiple sub-roles, becoming a "circle."

Because Holacracy is all about organizing the work, not the people, it leaves quite a bit of freedom for the people to self-organize around what roles they fill. Instead of getting organized as single nodes in the corporate hierarchy, people are left to act more like free agents, able to shop around and accept role assignments anywhere in the organizational structure, including filling several roles in many different parts of the organization at once. At Zappos, for example, that freedom enabled Matt, an employee originally from the social media team, to, in the words of one of his colleagues, "also become a meaningful part of many cross-cutting initiatives, like internal communications, progression and development systems, and Holacracy facilitation, in ways he wouldn't have been able to before."

Roles and Accountabilities

Consider your experience in a conventional organization: to whom are you accountable? The traditional answer is "my boss" or "my manager," but of course there are many others who count on you—your coworkers, your customers, perhaps investors or other stakeholders. A much more useful question is *"What* are those people counting on you *for?"* Each of the parties has different specific activities they are counting on you to own and to effectively manage, and clarity about these accountabilities is critical to the smooth running of an organization. More often than not this remains implicit. If things are running smoothly and our expectations are in alignment, then that's just fine. But too often, different people have different ideas about what each of them ought to be owning and doing, and this lack of clarity leads to all sorts of interpersonal friction and politics.

For example, I may want to send out an email with a link to our latest training information, and I'm counting on one of my coworkers to have updated the website. But if that coworker has a different idea of what he is accountable for, and only updates the website once a month, I may find that the information I need to send out is not online yet. The traditional management chain is irrelevant here; if we have different ideas of what he should be accountable for, our expectations will conflict.

WARNING SIGNS

Do any of these symptoms show up in your organization? If so, you may be suffering from a lack of clarity around roles and accountabilities.

- mistrust and frustration between coworkers
- critical tasks being "missed"
- lots of meetings with much discussion to reach consensus on things
- emails flying around with many people cc'd, often for unclear reasons
- people check in with everyone before making decisions, and expect that others will too
- people have lots of ideas about what "we" should do ... but "we" doesn't do it

When we have different expectations of each other, important tasks are dropped and everyone's frustrated. We feel let down by each other, we feel unfairly blamed, we mistrust, or we overstep our own roles in order to compensate, treading on other people's toes. No number of trust-building or team-building exercises can fix these problems, because these are often much less personal than they may feel—they result not from personal betrayal, mistrust, or insensitivity, but from a misalignment in our understanding of what we can count on each other for. They are a symptom of lack of clarity. To get to clarity, we must first let go of the idea that others should align with our implicit expectations (or anyone else's). This requires an effective governance process, which itself is documented explicitly, not wielded implicitly. The Holacracy governance process generates clarity by defining explicit roles with explicit accountabilities, which grant explicit authority, and then continuously evolves these definitions to integrate learning and align with the organization's ever-changing reality. This removes power from the vague and unspoken norms and instead vests it in a clear and documented process, and the expectations and authorities that result.

This can be a little uncomfortable at first. Shereef Bishay, the founder of the educational company Dev Bootcamp, put it succinctly: "The explicitness that Holacracy creates is uncivilized." Bishay was pointing to how accustomed we can get, in "civilized" society, to being vague and indirect. When things get really clear and concrete, it can feel awkward at first. But as clarity grows, trust is often a natural outcome. Over time, the organizational culture becomes more and more free of people using politics as a means of influence, simply because generating clarity through governance is more effective. An explicit structure of authorities and expectations also helps to differentiate between the people working in the organization and the functions or roles they fill. Decoupling these often fused elements is one key result of an effective Holacracy practice.

Differentiating Role and Soul

When a meeting with my partners at HolacracyOne results in my adding items to my task list, none of us thinks of those tasks as being assigned to "Brian." Instead, we might speak of a task being assigned to "Trainer," or "Program Design," or "Finance"—each of which is a role that I fill. Similarly, I may find myself referring to my partners not by their names, but as "Marketing" or "Website Director" or "Training Operations." This is not something we ever specifically decided to do; it started happening naturally. It may seem like a strange way to talk to the people I work with every day, but it's actually quite clarifying, and it points to a fundamental shift that Holacracy enables: the differentiation of people and roles, or "role and soul," as I like to put it.

In our modern organizational culture, individuals and the roles they fill are largely fused, and that fusion limits both the people and the organization in many ways. For example, often it is hard to separate emotions about people from emotions about the roles they fill. Sometimes the conflicts we have in organizational life are actually clashes of the roles involved, but we mistake them for clashes between the people filling those roles. Such conflicts become unnecessarily personal, and when we try to resolve them by smoothing over the human relationships, we miss the opportunity to clarify the underlying organizational "role-ationships"—a term I use to mean the relationship between our roles and what those roles need and want of each other, separate from our personal connection.

For example, if you fill the role of Business Development in an organization, you may be accountable for cultivating key client prospects, and you understand the importance of doing so in social settings. Yet you may clash with the person filling the Finance role, who demands itemized expense reports and questions the need for so many business lunches. You may feel affronted by her constant needling; it seems to you that she doesn't trust or like you. In fact, the conflict isn't personal—you are both just "energizing" your roles and "enacting" your accountabilities, as we often phrase it in Holacracy. The tension arises from a clash of priorities or expectations between these two roles, and the opportunity here is to clarify what it makes sense to expect of each role for the sake of the broader purpose.

Holacracy focuses on clearly differentiating individuals from the roles they fill. The organization's structure is defined by the roles the organization needs to pursue its purpose, without reference to the particular individuals in the organization. The people come in later, to fill or energize those roles. With roles defined around what is needed for the organization's purpose, we can then look at our available talent and assign the best fit for each role. Most of us will fill multiple roles quite naturally. In our personal lives, we are always filling multiple roles; one individual might be a parent, a spouse, a child, a teacher, and a student. Each of these roles comes with different expectations and responsibilities. In the same way, in an organization, one human being can fill multiple roles. At Holacracy-One, I fill about thirty roles, among them those I mentioned before: Trainer, Program Design, and Finance.

To facilitate clear and concrete role definitions, the Holacracy constitution defines a role as consisting of three specific elements: a "purpose" to express; possibly one or more "domains" to control; and a set of "accountabilities" to enact. Some roles will have all three of these parts, though often roles will start out with only a purpose or just a single accountability and evolve from there. A purpose tells us why the role exists: what it aims to achieve. A domain (of which there may be several) specifies something the role has the *exclusive* authority to control on behalf of the organization—in other words, this role's "property," which no other role can mess with. And each accountability is an ongoing activity that the role has the authority to perform and is expected to perform or otherwise manage for the organization. This coupling of authority with accountability helps avoid the situation we often see, in which people are held responsible for something they don't have the authority to actually do. Accountabilities are phrased beginning with a verb ending in "-ing," to indicate that they are not single projects but continuing activities. We'll examine the intersection among these three elements in more depth at the end of the next chapter.

SAMPLE ROLE DEFINITION

Every role can have a purpose, domains, and accountabilities.

Role: Marketing

Purpose: Lots of buzz about our company and its services

Domains:

- The company's mailing list and social media accounts
- Content on the company's public website

Accountabilities:
- Building relationships with potential customers in kets defined by the Marketing Strategy role
- Promoting and highlighting the organization's services to potential customers via the Web and social media channels
- Triaging speaking invitations and other PR opportunities sent to the organization, and routing good opportunities to the Spokesperson role

Roles in Holacracy are dynamic, living things that change over time. Unlike traditional job descriptions, which are often vague, theoretical, and soon outdated, Holacracy role definitions are based on the reality of what activities are experienced as useful in the organization, and they stay in sync with that evolving reality. Holacracy's governance process allows for the continual clarification and refinement of roles on the basis of actual tensions that arise, rather than on the basis of abstract predictions. Let's say you experience a tension in one of your roles because you were expecting a coworker to perform some function, and she fails to deliver. Holacracy's rules and processes will force you to face the question: "Is this an explicit accountability of her role, or is it your implicit expectation?" It may seem like a perfectly natural and reasonable expectation to you, but in Holacracy, if it's not an explicit accountability of one of her roles, you have no right to expect it of her. However, if you feel it's something you *should* be able to count on her for, you can bring a proposal to the next governance meeting that the task in question be made an explicit accountability of her role. (I'll discuss this process in more detail in the next chapter, on governance.)

When we have real clarity about roles and the role-ationships at play, we can find relief from many common frustrations of organizational life. We no longer need meetings at which we discuss every decision, as we know what authority we have and what other roles we may need to involve and why. That means we also no longer need to copy everyone on emails or check in with everyone before making a decision. When we do engage in a group discussion, we can do so without creating an expectation of consensus, because everyone is crystal clear on which roles have authority to make which decisions. We also know what we can reasonably expect from others and what others can expect from us as we go about our work and exercise authority together. Organizational clarity creates an authentic distribution of power, freeing each of us to be a good leader when we're filling a role and need to balance input with expediency, and a good follower when another role owns a decision and shuts down discussion to make a judgment call.

Circles

Roles, in the way I've just described them, are like the cells of the organization. Now let's look at the overall organizational structure by which roles are grouped and integrated. A typical org chart looks like an upside-down tree, with each node representing a person (or a "position," but when positions are matched one to one with persons, it becomes much the same). A holarchy, however, looks like a series of nested circles, like cells within organs within organisms. In a holarchy, each part or holon is not subjugated to those above it, but retains autonomy, individual authority, and wholeness. So we've got a holarchy of roles grouped within circles, which are themselves grouped within broader circles, all the way up until the biggest circle contains the entire organization. This circle is called the "Anchor Circle" in the constitution. Every circle and role within the holarchy retains real autonomy and authority as a cohesive, whole entity itself, and also has real responsibilities as a part of a larger entity.

Despite each circle's fundamental autonomy, its decisions and actions are not fully independent of others. Remember, each circle is a holon—both a self-organizing entity in its own right and a part of a larger circle. As a part, it shares its environment with the other functions and sub-circles of that broader circle. So a circle that behaves as if it were fully autonomous will harm the system, just as a cell in the body that disregards the larger system becomes cancer. The needs of other circles must be taken into account in the self-organizing process. In Holacracy, this is accomplished by defining the accountabilities and constraints each circle must also align with—and those other circles have a say in that, as we'll see in the next chapter.

Basic Circle Structure

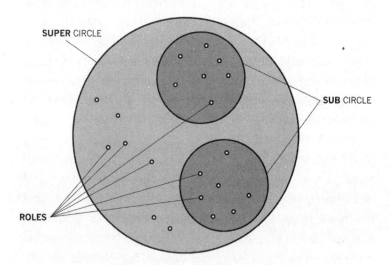

This structure captures the core shift necessary for Holacracy's distribution of authority—from a hierarchy of people directing people, to a holarchy of organizational functions assigned to roles and circles. And this is a critical difference: a shift not simply in the *type* of structure, from hierarchy to holarchy, but in *what* we're structuring in the first place. Holacracy moves from structuring the people to structuring the organization's roles and functions. More specifically, instead of structuring a simple power relationship between people—who can give orders to whom—Holacracy structures where work lives within the overall system, and it elucidates the boundaries between the various entities doing that work. Because of this, I think it can be misleading to claim either "Holacracy is flat" or "Holacracy is hierarchical"; Holacracy uses a different type of hierarchy than we're used to, for a different purpose.

Making this shift means more than just renaming your existing departments or calling your project teams circles. A circle is not a group of people but a group of roles, and it is also, in a sense, a really big role itself, with a single cohesive purpose to express, some accountabilities to enact, and possibly some domains to control. The roles a circle contains are a breakdown of what's needed to express its overall purpose, enact its accountabilities, and control its domains. A circle has the autonomy and authority to self-organize and to coordinate and integrate the work of all the roles it contains. This self-organization happens in the circle's governance meetings, a subject I'll turn to in the next chapter.

The work of circles can vary wildly in both type and scale. Some circles implement specific projects; others manage a department or a business line, or perform particular support functions, or deal with overall business operations. Some circles are small and narrowly focused, while larger circles may embrace several fully contained circles. For example, an organization may offer a particular service; the multiple roles involved in that service's delivery may be grouped into a circle to govern the overall delivery process. That circle might itself be grouped with others into a larger circle that integrates other functions parallel to delivery, such as sales, marketing, and support.

Sometimes a circle forms when the accountabilities of one role grow complex enough that they require further differentiation to be effectively enacted. A small start-up might begin with a single overall Marketing role, filled by one person; as the company grows, its marketing needs may differentiate, so that they now call for multiple intertwined roles filled by multiple people. Thus the Marketing role expands into a Marketing circle, to further break down that work. The roles it contains might now include Social Media, Advertising, Web Marketing, and Brand Development. Eventually, the Social Media role might become too much for one person to fill; in that case, its accountabilities may be divided among two or three roles, so Social Media becomes a circle of its own, a "sub-circle" within the Marketing "super-circle." Whatever a circle's level of scale and focus, the same basic rules apply.

Lead Links and Rep Links

Whenever a circle contains sub-circles, the super-circle and each sub-circle are linked via two special roles, which straddle the boundary between the connected circles, like channels across a cell's membrane. These roles, called links, take part in the governance and operational processes of both connected circles and allow feedback and tension processing to flow across circle boundaries. The "Lead Link" is appointed by the super-circle to represent its needs in the sub-circle. A lead link holds the perspective and functions needed to align the sub-circle with the purpose, strategy, and needs of its broader context. The other link, called a "Representative Link" or "Rep Link," is elected by the members of the sub-circle, and represents the sub-circle within its super-circle. This rep link role is quite different from anything we're used to in a modern organization. A rep link helps make the super-circle a healthy environment for the sub-circle, by carrying key perspectives from the sub-circle to the super-circle's governance and operations. Rep links bring frontline feedback to the broader context, while guarding the autonomy and sustainability of the sub-circle within that environment. To fulfill their functions, both links may take part in the governance and operations of both connected circles.

To take up the Social Media example from the preceding section: within the Social Media circle there's a lead link, whose function might include bringing her awareness of the broader Marketing circle's strategy and messaging to the activities of the Social Media circle, to ensure they stay aligned. The Social Media circle has also elected a rep link, who would be listening for issues surfacing within the Social Media team that should inform how other parts of marketing are done (or not done), so these issues can be raised in the broader Marketing circle and addressed there. The rep link might also need to ensure that Marketing's overall messaging strategy is compatible with the nature of social media, as distinguished from more traditional media outlets. Both links would also show up in the Marketing circle's governance meetings, where both would represent the Social Media circle as a whole, each with a slightly different perspective.

This linking of circles and their contained sub-circles continues throughout the organizational holarchy, one layer at a time, creating bidirectional pathways for alignment and feedback.

The role of lead link serves a key function in every circle, but don't confuse it with the role of a traditional manager. The lead link is not managing the circle members (who may actually fill roles in many circles anyway, with many different lead

Linking Circles

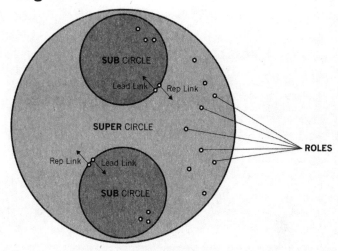

links). It is not the lead link's job to direct the team, or to take care of all the tensions felt by those in the circle. As a lead link, you are not managing the people; you are representing the circle as a whole and its purpose within the broader environment of the organization. The best metaphor I've found for the lead link role is that if the circle is a cell, the lead link is the cell membrane. As lead link, rather than directing the action, you hold the space within which the purpose of the circle can be fulfilled, and you keep out issues and concerns that are not within the scope of that circle. You also act as an interface at the circle's boundary when needed, routing incoming information or requests to appropriate roles, and bringing resources into the circle and directing them to the most important functions, roles, or projects within the circle. You are on alert for any lack of clarity in the circle around what role handles what work and makes what decisions, and you work to achieve that clarity through the governance process. In a new circle, the lead link role is an entrepreneurial role—you're actively building a structure to achieve a purpose, and you will need to try different approaches, see what works, and adapt—all on behalf of the circle itself and its purpose.

ROLE DESCRIPTION FOR LEAD LINK

Purpose
The lead link holds the purpose of the overall circle.

Domains
- Role assignments within the circle

Accountabilities
- Structuring the governance of the circle to express its purpose and enact its accountabilities
- Assigning partners to the circle's roles; monitoring the fit; offering feedback to enhance fit; and reassigning roles to other partners when useful for enhancing fit
- Allocating the circle's resources across its various projects and/or roles
- Establishing priorities and strategies for the circle
- Defining metrics for the circle

The lead link also inherits the circle's domains and accountabilities, but only when they aren't delegated to another role or process.

The lead link does have some accountabilities that will be familiar to seasoned managers, such as assigning people to roles and setting priorities. Yet when those managers step into lead link roles, their challenge will be to understand the differences and the limits of their authority. Ultimately, all roles created in a Holacracy-powered company have real authority that no one else can trump, and lead link is just another role, with its own authorities and limits. Anna McGrath, a Holacracy coach, told me a story about a meeting she was participating in at Pantheon Enterprises, an eco-chemical manufacturing company that she was helping with Holacracy. The lead link of one particular circle was the company's leader and founder, a former nuclear engineer with a wealth of experience. Also in that circle was his stepson, Steven, a twenty-two-year-old who was filling the role of Production Assistant. At a certain point, Steven made a decision in his role, which the lead link disagreed with, suggesting a different approach. Anna remarked upon how the young man "was not rude or obnoxious, but simply stated that he had autonomy over this decision, and no more time was wasted. To me this was an example of how anyone in an organization running with Holacracy, from the most junior to the most senior person, can own his or her power and authority in alignment with clear accountabilities, and have others respect his or her sovereignty."

The story illustrates one way a lead link's power is constrained by the constitution. A lead link may be able to remove someone from a role, but she has no authority to fire someone, determine compensation, or define new roles and expectations for people outside of the governance process. And while a lead link can expect a role filler in her circle to prioritize one project over another at her request, she cannot demand that he accept a specific project in the first place. That role filler still gets to assess whether a project requested by a lead link fits his role's purpose or accountabilities; if it doesn't, he can simply decline, and even if it does he can still dismiss it in favor of an alternative outcome he feels is a more appropriate way to express his role.

A question around this arose recently in one of our client organizations. A circle focused on internal learning decided they needed a role to capture and share best practices for a new tool they were using, so they created a role with an accountability for "documenting and sharing best practices from affiliates and others." On that basis, the lead link of the circle asked the role filler to create an internal wiki where employees could share best practices. This was something he (or anyone in the circle) had the right to request, but the question that surfaced was whether the role filler had to accept the project and create the requested wiki.

The answer, under Holacracy's rules, is a clear no. While a role filler does have a duty to do something to express her accountability, she doesn't have to accept a specific project as the way to do it. Perhaps in this case the role filler had been researching the pros and cons of internal wikis versus public-facing blogs, and had come to the conclusion that her role would be better served by introducing a blog, to allow comments and support from outside the team. As the role filler, she has the autonomy to lead her role and choose how she expresses its accountabilities. The lead link can't override this; his power extends only to getting the right people into roles, and then to prioritizing work across the whole circle. If there's a role unfilled in the circle, or a function of the circle that isn't yet held by any role, then the lead link acts as the catch-all, taking responsibility for anything that might otherwise fall through the cracks—but only until he can create an appropriate role in governance, and then assign someone to fill it.

The role of rep link also serves a key function for every circle, and it's not just a "second" link, but a different function from the lead link altogether. If the lead link is mostly a membrane around the cell, the rep link is a direct channel from within the core of the cell out through that membrane. He or she provides rapid feedback from the perspective of someone who really knows what's going on at "street level," and it's the rep link's accountability—not the lead link's—to channel tensions out into the broader circle if they are seen to be limiting a sub-circle and can't be resolved locally. For example, if the Social Media circle is having trouble effectively promoting the company's products because the Marketing circle's messaging guidelines are too much of a hard sell for the more conversational environments of Twitter and Facebook, the rep link can bring this tension to the Marketing circle's next governance meeting. Here, she can propose a solution, such as adding an accountability to the Brand Manager role to consult a Social Media circle member when creating messaging guidelines.

Rep links help to free lead links from dealing with the tensions their circle members have about the broader company and its other circles, leaving the lead link more time and energy to focus on moving the circle forward in other ways.

ROLE DESCRIPTION FOR REP LINK

Purpose
Within the super-circle, the rep link holds the purpose of the sub-circle; within the sub-circle, the rep link's purpose is: tensions relevant to process in the super-circle channeled out and resolved.

Accountabilities
- Removing constraints within the broader organization that limit the sub-circle
- Seeking to understand tensions conveyed by sub-circle circle members, and discerning those appropriate to process in the super-circle
- Providing visibility to the super-circle into the health of the sub-circle, including reporting on any metrics or checklist items assigned to the whole sub-circle

Cross Links

In addition to lead links and rep links, a third type of link is used in Holacracy's structure: the much more rare "Cross Link." Whereas lead links and rep links connect circles when one contains the other, cross links connect parallel circles, or those otherwise removed from each other in the organization's holarchy. Adding a cross link between two circles provides a direct channel for processing tensions within one circle that were sensed in another circle, even one far removed in the organizational holarchy, without having to go through the usual lead link or rep link channels. In most cases, cross links are not needed because those two circles are contained by a larger circle at some level, so that a question around how the two sub-circles relate to each other can be resolved in that larger circle. For example, at HolacracyOne, our Service Delivery circle and our Outreach circle are both contained within our General Company circle. At times, we need to figure out something about how those two circles relate to each other and what they can expect from each other, but there is no need for a cross link because we can process those issues in our General Company circle's governance meetings.

However, if two sub-circles have so much integration to do that it would become a distraction for the larger circle, it makes more sense to appoint a cross link from one of those circles into the other, so that they can work out their issues directly without bringing them to the larger circle. Cross links can also be useful when there is a relationship between two radically different parts of the organization. For example, one company I worked with created a cross link from the sales department into a specific team delivering work for clients, which was many circles removed in the company's overall organizational structure. Despite their structural distance, there was a natural need to process tensions between them, given the unique perspective of the sales role in the overall client relationship, and how relevant the client's delivery experience is to the next big sale. The cross link allows for easier and faster processing of tensions. Again, cross links are rarely needed and easy to misuse, especially in organizations new to Holacracy, but as the practice becomes more advanced, in specific cases they can help. They also have an important role to play in a Holacracy-powered board, which I'll discuss more in Chapter 8.

Elected versus Assigned Roles

For the purpose of conducting meetings, as we will see in the following chapters, two specific roles must be filled in each circle: the "Facilitator" and the "Secretary." These roles, as well as that of the rep link, are filled via an election conducted in a circle's governance meeting, using the "Integrative Election Process" defined in detail in the constitution. Elected roles are given a term when elected (often one year), but any circle member may call for a new election at any time.

Aside from these three elected roles, all roles in a circle are filled by the circle's lead link, who assigns the role to someone available to do work for the organization. The Holacracy constitution refers to these people as "partners" of the organization, whether they're technically employees, contractors, business partners, or in some other legal relationship. A partner assigned to a role is free to resign from that assignment at any point, unless he or she has agreed otherwise, for example as a condition of a work contract with the organization. Even lead link roles are filled this way. To take up our example from earlier, the Marketing circle's lead link will assign someone to fill the role of lead link to the Social Media circle, and that lead link will then assign people to fill the various roles created by the Social Media circle—except for the circle's rep link, facilitator, and secretary, which are always elected.

What Circles Do

The activities of a circle are all driven by the tensions sensed by those filling its roles and doing its work—the "circle members." Circle members include anyone filling a particular role in the circle, as well as the lead link appointed from the super-circle and any rep links connected into the circle from its sub-circles.

How circle members process tensions depends on each particular tension. Some tensions are best resolved by taking action (operations), while others require changing the pattern or structure by which the circle functions (governance). To facilitate the processing of tensions in different ways, at least two different types of meetings are held regularly within each circle, and each meeting type has its own process and rules of the game. We will unpack the specifics of these meeting processes in the chapters that follow; below is a brief overview to get us started.

In "Governance Meetings," circle members refine the structure of the circle based on the basis of new information and experiences that arise during day-to-day work. This results in clear understanding of roles, their activities, and their relationships, as well as of circle policies. Governance meetings in mature circles are often held every month or two, but I recommend two meetings per month for most new circles and for those with many members who are new to Holacracy.

In "Tactical Meetings," circle members use a fast-paced forum to deal with their ongoing operations, synchronize team members, and triage any difficulties that are preventing progress. This results in clear understanding of projects and next-actions to be taken. Tactical meetings typically happen weekly, although every other week works for some circles.

Practice Makes Perfect

I hope that these opening chapters have given you a sense of the paradigm shift that Holacracy represents. If there is one thing I aim to have communicated, it is that Holacracy is not simply a bolt-on technique that you can add on top of your existing structure, but a fundamental shift in the way power works and the way a company is organized. This is good news, because the social technology underpinning modern companies has become the primary constraint on their evolution and adaptability, trapping them in an industrial-age design. Many of us sense this, but have no option other than to try to be better, more empowering leaders within the old structures. Holacracy offers a viable alternative.

The chapters that follow describe the practice of Holacracy and its unique rules of the game for dynamic, purpose-driven organizations. I use the term "practice" because Holacracy is something you can only fully understand through doing and applying it regularly, like exercise, speaking a new language, or playing a musical instrument. To really provide benefits, Holacracy must be applied and practiced until it becomes habitual. Like all new habits, it will feel awkward at first, but if you continue to practice it will eventually become second nature.

PART TWO

EVOLUTION
AT PLAY:
PRACTICING
HOLACRACY

4

GOVERNANCE

If we can agree that the economic problem of society is mainly one of rapid adaptation to changes in the particular circumstances of time and place, it would seem to follow that the ultimate decisions must be left to the people who are familiar with these circumstances, who know directly of the relevant changes and of the resources immediately available to meet them.

—F. A. HAYEK, "The Use of Knowledge in Society"

When you watch a professional sports team moving fluidly down the court or field, interacting, passing, defending, and scoring, are you thinking about the rules of the game? If it's a game you're familiar with, probably not—no more than the players are. The intricate set of rules and processes that keep the game going have faded into the background. Without them, of course, the game would descend into chaotically kicking a ball around. When everyone in the game has embraced the rules and agreed to play by them, they become habit—unnoticed, implicit, and automatic. That is, until the rules are broken. The minute a player violates a rule, its existence springs into the conscious awareness of the athletes on the field, the coaches, the referees, and the fans. The whistle blows, the card is waved, and appropriate action is taken, so that the game can return to its smooth flow and the rules can fade into the background once again.

Holacracy works in much the same way. When you replace top-down leadership with a process, that process needs to be robust and sophisticated enough to keep everyone aligned and unified as they navigate the complexity of their daily business. The meeting processes that define the day-to-day running of Holacracy are like the plays of a game: once everyone follows the rules, they become second nature. But in the beginning, much like a child learning to play a sport, you will find yourself having to remember and refer to the rules again and again. They may feel cumbersome, or restrictive, but they exist for a reason. If your seven-year-old son asked why he couldn't just pick up the ball and run with it while playing soccer, you would explain to him that the game simply wouldn't work if everyone did that. The same is true of Holacracy. In this chapter and in Chapter 6, I will explain quite complex and detailed rules and processes for conducting governance meetings. Many people I work with have never been in meetings that are structured to this degree, and often they do not see the benefit at first. To some, the very words "rules" and "structure" have only negative connotations. Yet, as David Allen puts it, "There is no freedom without discipline, no vision without a form. . . . If there were no lines painted on the road, you wouldn't be free to let your mind wander and be creative while you drive. You'd be too busy hoping no one hits you. But if there were too many lanes and restrictions and rules, you'd have traffic moving much slower than it should, as everyone was trying to pay attention to the right place to be."[10]

When you begin practicing Holacracy, you may feel as if you are stuck in that slow-moving traffic, having to pay more attention than you are accustomed to. I assure you that if you and your colleagues continue to practice Holacracy, following the rules as diligently as a young team practicing soccer, you will sooner or later find that you have forgotten all about the rules and processes, and instead are able to marvel at the fluid, spontaneous, efficient tension-processing system that your team has become. Eventually, you may even take the new state for granted.

Back in the days with my software company, I remember a governance meeting of our General Company circle that had been scheduled for a two-hour slot. In this meeting, we changed our salary system quite dramatically, restructured part of the organization in a major way, and adopted a few new policies that affected the whole organization. None of these topics was discussed or "socialized" before the meeting. We finished half an hour early, and everybody involved had fully bought into the path forward (including frontline staff there as rep links from our sub-circles). As the meeting was closing, the facilitator offered an apology for being a little off his game: he felt that the meeting had taken longer than necessary. Others agreed. It wasn't until we were leaving the room that it occurred to me how unusual this was compared to most organizations—look what we had accomplished in ninety minutes. But in an organization that has mastered Holacracy, this rapid restructuring and integration is the norm.

Governance Meetings

When I introduce Holacracy in a training workshop, I don't spend much time explaining the meeting processes in theory. Instead, I break people into groups, assign them roles in a fictional business, and guide them through a series of simulations. In the process, all their questions and objections arise naturally and can be answered; more importantly, participants get a taste of what the rules and structure make possible. In this chapter, I will endeavor to give you both an overview and an experience of a Holacracy-style governance meeting, as well as I can in a book. I'll assign you a role and guide you step-by-step through a meeting scenario. While nothing can quite substitute for direct participation, I hope that this taste will leave you hungry for an opportunity to experience it for yourself.

Of the two spheres Holacracy addresses—governance and operations—I will start with governance, as all of the organization's operations rest on top of the structure built through governance. Governance is fundamental; it is the seat of the organization's power, and all authorities and expectations flow from the governance process. The rules of a governance meeting are nuanced and strict, and often the most awkward to follow at first. But they are critical. Governance deals with deep issues by using an "integrative" process to gather and consider people's input, without relying on a single leader to arbitrate, and we need a very specific format to make that process work. Governance meetings happen in every circle, often monthly, to refine the operating structure of the circle.

ROLE DESCRIPTION FOR FACILITATOR

Purpose
Circle governance and operational practices that are aligned with the constitution.

Accountabilities
- Facilitating the circle's constitutionally required meetings
- Auditing the meetings and records of sub-circles as needed, and initiating the restorative process defined in the constitution upon discovering a process breakdown

ROLE DESCRIPTION FOR SECRETARY

Purpose
Steward and stabilize the circle's formal records and record-keeping process.

Domains
- All constitutionally required records of the circle

Accountabilities
- Scheduling the circle's required meetings, and notifying all core circle members of scheduled times and locations
- Capturing the outputs of the circle's required meetings, and maintaining a compiled view of the circle's current governance, checklist items, and metrics
- Interpreting governance and the constitution upon request

Governance meetings have very particular functions, and the constitution expressly limits the allowed "outputs" of a governance meeting—the types of activities that can be included and the decisions that can be made. A facilitator's failure to understand and adhere to this restriction will undermine the entire system of Holacracy. Specifically, the allowed activities in a governance meeting are

- creating, amending, or removing roles within the circle
- creating, amending, or removing policies governing the circle's domain
- electing circle members to fill elected roles (facilitator, secretary, and rep link)
- creating, amending, or dissolving sub-circles

With practice, circle members will learn what kinds of issues are best addressed through governance changes. If a key task has been consistently falling through the cracks, and it becomes

clear that it needs to be added to the accountabilities of a particular role, that's a likely target for a governance meeting. If the
relationship between two roles is unclear, creating tension and
communication problems, that can be clarified in a governance
meeting. If the individual filling a role wants the authority to
make certain decisions, or place limits on others' authority, that,
too, can be brought to the table. Governance meetings are *not*
the place to be dealing with the marketing strategy, the product
offerings for next year, or any other execution-oriented decisions
facing the team. Those are operational questions, and should be
addressed day to day outside of meetings, or, sometimes, in a
tactical meeting. I'll explain that process later.

A Taste of Governance

Let's walk through a governance meeting simulation. This scenario resembles one I often use in introductory workshops,
and we'll start with a simple example so you can see how the
process works. The participants in our fictional meeting are
novices in Holacracy, so you'll see some struggles and learning points that new practitioners commonly encounter in their
first governance meetings after they adopt the system.

Without further ado, welcome to the Better Widgets Company, a small business that manufactures and sells widgets—
for all your widget needs. Better Widgets is composed of a
General Company circle and two sub-circles: a Widget Production circle and a Marketing circle. In addition to a lead link
and rep link for each of the two sub-circles, the General Company circle includes the roles of Widget Design, Customer Support, Widget Sales, Website Manager, and Finance, each filled
by just a single person. As I said, it's a small company.

The governance meeting you are about to participate in is
happening in the General Company circle (GCC). Everyone

BETTER WIDGETS COMPANY

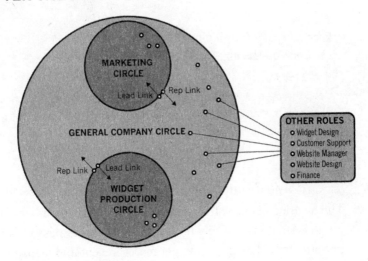

who fills a role in that circle is invited to participate, as are the lead links and rep links connecting the GCC with each of its sub-circles. For this meeting, you are filling the role of Widget Sales. Below is a quick overview of the steps you'll use in the governance meeting process.

GOVERNANCE MEETING PROCESS

1. Check-in Round
One at a time, each participant has space to call out distractions and orient to the meeting.

2. Administrative Concerns
Quickly address any logistical matters, such as time allotted for the meeting and any planned breaks.

3. Agenda Building
Participants add agenda items, using just one or two words per item. Each agenda item represents one tension to process. Facilitator captures them in a list.

4. Process Each Agenda Item Using the Integrative Decision-Making Process
Each agenda item is addressed, one at a time, using the Integrative Decision-Making Process.

5. Closing Round
Once the agenda is complete or the meeting is nearing its scheduled end, the facilitator gives each person space to share a closing reflection about the meeting.

1. Check-in Round

The meeting opens with a check-in round. Each member of the circle is invited to briefly notice and share what has got his or her attention. The goal is to get more present and focused, by making conscious whatever distractions are present—thought streams, physical discomforts, or emotional states. A check-in also provides context for your teammates, so that if you're not showing up with your usual grace, they have some idea what's going on and what to attribute it to.

Almost anything can be said in this round. One person is feeling under the weather. The circle member who fills the Customer Support role just dropped her dog off at the vet and is worried about him. The circle member who fills the role of Widget Design is distracted by a looming deadline the following day and wants to get the meeting over quickly. Others are simply feeling good, or have nothing particular on their minds. You don't have to share any detail in this round that you would be uncomfortable with, but becoming conscious of what's on your mind and putting it out on the table is a powerful way to bring everyone into the present moment.

The check-in is not the place for any kind of discussion. In fact, the job of the facilitator is to protect this "sacred space," and not allow any cross talk or response whatsoever. This may be challenging. Resist the instinct to express empathy or to offer advice; this is not the moment for it. This rule also makes it safe for people to be unguarded, knowing that they will not invite unwanted response or intrusion on their personal lives. Once the check-in round is complete, the team should be more present and focused, ready to move on to the next step in the process.

2. Administrative Concerns

Very briefly, the facilitator addresses any practical constraints on the meeting. For example, only ninety minutes is allotted for the meeting, and one circle member needs to leave early. This step should stay brief and purely administrative; don't let it become a space for anything more.

3. Agenda Building

At this point, it's time to build the agenda for the meeting. Specific agenda items are not pre-established for this meeting; instead, the agenda is built on the fly. Any circle member may add an item to the agenda to attempt to process a tension into amended governance for the circle. The agenda-building step is not the time for people to *explain* their tensions, however. All that is needed for the agenda is a one- or two-word placeholder; anything more will be cut off by the facilitator. For example, the Marketing lead link has a tension related to sending out email newsletters, because the company website that her newsletters link to often doesn't include up-to-date information about newly launched widgets. But this is not the moment for Marketing to explain all of that. All she does is add something like "website updates" to the agenda as a placeholder for that tension.

In your role as Widget Sales, you have a tension about the price of the company's widgets, which you've heard from customers is too high. You add "widget prices" to the agenda.

Once all desired agenda items have been added, the facilitator moves the group to processing them, one at a time, using the "Integrative Decision-Making Process."

4. Integrative Decision Making

INTEGRATIVE DECISION-MAKING PROCESS IN BRIEF

Present Proposal   *Who Speaks: Proposer Only, Unless Help Is Requested*

The proposer has space to describe a tension and state a proposal to resolve it, with no discussion. The proposer can optionally request discussion just to help craft a proposal, but not to build consensus or integrate concerns.

Clarifying Questions *Who Speaks: Anyone Asks, Proposer Answers; Repeat*

Anyone can ask a clarifying question to seek information or understanding. The proposer can respond or say "not specified." No reactions or dialogue allowed.

Reaction Round   *Who Speaks: Everyone Except Proposer, One at a Time*

Each person is given space to react to the proposal as they see fit; reactions must be made as first- or third-person comments. No discussion or responses.

Amend and Clarify *Who Speaks: Proposer Only*

The proposer can optionally clarify the intent of the proposal further or amend the proposal based on the reactions, or just move on. No discussion allowed.

Objection Round   *Who Speaks: Everyone Including Proposer, One at a Time*

The facilitator asks: "Do you see any reasons why adopting this proposal would cause harm or move us backward?" (an "objection"). Objections are stated, tested, and captured without discussion; the proposal is adopted if none surface.

Integration   *Who Speaks: Mostly Objector and Proposer;*
                       Others Can Help

Focus on each objection, one at a time. The goal is to craft an amended proposal that would not cause the objection, but that would still address the proposer's tension. Once all are integrated, go back to the Objection Round with the new proposal.

As Widget Sales, you've added the agenda item "widget prices," and now it's time to process it. First, you are invited to **present your proposal**, and, if you want, the tension that prompted it. If you do not have a proposal, you can share the tension and invite an open discussion to help you craft a proposal; but in our scenario, you know what you think the solution to your tension should be: "I propose that we reduce the price of our basic widget by fifty percent." By way of explanation, you share the tension: "I'm consistently hearing from our customers that the price is too high. That basic widget is supposed to help sell our more sophisticated widgets, and if it's too expensive to entice new customers it's not serving its function." The secretary captures the wording of your proposal for everyone to see.

With your proposal on the table, the facilitator moves to the next step and makes space for anyone to ask **clarifying questions**, for the sole purpose of understanding your proposal or the tension behind it. This is still not a moment for discussion or response. When Finance tries to exclaim "Why fifty percent? That's a ridiculous suggestion!" the facilitator cuts him off before he's even finished the sentence, as his tone immediately indicates he is conveying a reaction or an opinion, not simply a clarifying question. Or suppose the lead link asks, "Don't you think a lower price could hurt our profitability?" The facilitator will disallow this and cut it off, because it's a reaction disguised as a question. Anything that conveys an opinion to the proposer is probably a reaction; clarifying questions are solely for seeking information from the proposer. When the Widget Design role filler asks whether the proposal refers only to the single-widget price or also to bulk prices, that's a fair question. However, as the proposer, you can always respond to a clarifying question by simply saying, "Not specified in the proposal," so you don't have to feel pressured to come up with answers to everything up front.

Once the clarifying questions die down, the facilitator moves to the next step, a **reaction round**, during which each person gets to air his or her reactions to the proposal. Almost anything goes, but neither cross talk nor responses to one another are allowed. Reactions might be "I completely agree—love the idea!" or "I think it's crazy!" Finance's comment that the pricing cut is ridiculous, which was disallowed when disguised as a clarifying question, is welcome in this round. Someone might have a different idea, or critique this particular way of addressing the original tension that gave rise to the proposal. Once again, none of the reactions is engaged with or responded to, no matter what they are. The reaction round proceeds around the room, one person at a time, with everyone except the proposer having one and only one turn to share reactions.

Once the reaction round is complete, the facilitator returns to you as the proposer, to give you a chance to **amend and clarify** the proposal as you see fit based on the questions or reactions. The facilitator also encourages you to be "selfish" on behalf of your role, and ignore the reactions that don't make sense to you. The goal of this step is not to integrate everyone's reactions, but just to make whatever changes would help you better address your tension. You also have the opportunity to clarify any misunderstandings or add any more data you think may help people better understand what you're proposing and why. Ultimately, as Widget Sales, you decide to clarify your intent for the pricing adjustment further, and to amend your proposal's wording to specify single-item price only.

With your modified proposal captured by the secretary, the facilitator moves to the **objection round** and asks each person, one at a time, if she or he sees any "objections" to your proposal—an objection being *a concrete reason why adopting the proposal would cause harm or move the circle backward*. Objections are stated without discussion or questions, and captured by the facilitator. If no objections surface, the proposal is adopted. In this instance, there is an objection from Finance, who says the widgets won't be profitable if the price is halved, and that that will cause harm. The facilitator captures the objection and moves on. Customer Support also raises an objection: "We need to consider the pricing of our long-term support services as well—they're also too expensive. We need a more cohesive review of our pricing strategy."

The facilitator pauses on this comment because it may be a related concern that should also be addressed, but it may not actually articulate a reason that the widget-pricing proposal would move the circle backward. "Is that a reason that this specific proposal would cause harm, or is that just something else we need to consider?" the facilitator asks. Customer Support realizes that it is the latter, so the objection is dropped, and Customer Support opts to add her tension to the agenda for processing in turn—we'll examine the reason for this further in Chapter 6. The facilitator continues the objection round and finds no further objections, except for one she raises herself: "Not valid governance output."

What does that mean? It means that the proposal in its current form is not actually something that a governance meeting can decide, under the terms of the constitution. Remember, governance is about defining and amending roles and setting policies. Deciding the specific pricing level for a service is an operational issue. Perhaps you already noticed this, and were wondering why I've chosen an example proposal that's invalid. I did so because it illustrates one of the most important first lessons to be learned as you adopt Holacracy: what governance is and what it is not. I also see examples like this all the time in facilitating new Holacracy practitioners, and it's one of the first challenges a new facilitator must learn how to address.

So what happens now? Does the facilitator just dismiss the proposal? Definitely not—that would be outside the scope of the facilitator's authority, and harmful to the process. In fact, the proposal is perfectly valid *input* to get the governance process rolling, just not valid *output*. When a proposal is brought in a form that's not valid for governance, it creates an opportunity to look deeper. This is also why the facilitator didn't simply stop the proposal at the beginning and redirect you to an operational meeting: to do so would have prevented the opportunity to discover whether there is in fact a governance issue underlying your tension, and there almost certainly is. If you knew exactly who is accountable for setting prices and who has the authority to change them, you probably wouldn't have felt the need to propose the decision to the whole group in the first place. But a quick check of the circle's governance records confirms that no one is explicitly accountable for this, and so more clarification is needed. What role has the authority to decide pricing, and what accountabilities are needed on that role? *That* is a governance issue.

And so, with that objection charted, the facilitator opens up the **integration** step of the process, and starts by focusing on that objection and asking, "What can we add to or amend in this proposal in order to address this objection?" An open discussion ensues, with the objector clarifying the objection if needed and offering possible amendments to avoid it, and the proposer considering whether those amendments would still address that original tension. In this case, the objection is clear: pricing is not a governance issue. So you enlist the help of the group to create a modified proposal that stays within the scope of governance but will still address your tension.

Create new role: Pricing Manager
Accountable for:
Researching and selecting profitable pricing models to reach
the target market defined by Marketing.

This new proposal no longer dictates the operational decision of lowering prices by 50 percent; instead, it defines the ongoing accountabilities and authorities needed to figure out the right operational decision. It's thus valid governance output, and the objector agrees that the modified proposal would resolve the objection.

With that objection checked off, the facilitator focuses on the other objection raised by Finance, about hurting profitability, but since the amended proposal no longer dictates a specific decision that objector quickly drops the objection, satisfied that there's no harm in empowering a Pricing Manager role to figure out the right profitable pricing model. With all objections either addressed or dropped, the facilitator cuts off the integration step and moves back to an objection round to check for objections to the amended proposal. Once no objections surface, the proposal is adopted as part of the formal governance of the circle, and a new role is thus created.

With your tension processed into meaningful new clarity, you sit back and relax, knowing that you can raise objections should any other proposal threaten to undo that forward progress. The other agenda items are processed and, as the clock approaches the end of the scheduled meeting time, the facilitator shifts the group into a **closing round,** giving each person the opportunity to share reflections about the meeting. Once again, each person speaks one at a time, with no discussion or response allowed, and the meeting is over once the last person has shared.

I hope this example has given you a glimpse of this often-invisible but foundational role of governance, and a sense of what Holacracy's governance meeting process is like. Among the range of possible proposals and integrations in a governance meeting, this was a fairly simple example. More complex proposals are sometimes needed to resolve a tension as well, with multiple proposed changes to multiple roles and policies; multiple objections, both valid and invalid, are often raised along the way. In Chapter 6, we will discuss how the validity of objections can be tested, as well as how to handle disruptive behaviors that threaten to derail the governance process. For now, just remember this: governance meetings are about evolving the pattern and structure of the organization—defining how we will work together—not about conducting specific business or making decisions about specific issues.

That's not to say we avoid all talk of operational issues in these meetings; governance proposals are typically inspired by specific operational needs or events, as in the example above. Whenever something hasn't gone as well as we may have liked, there may be an improvement waiting to be uncovered in a governance meeting. The key to generating valid governance output when operational matters are put forth is to pull the focus back from the specific issues to the underlying structure—to the roles at play, and to the purpose, accountabilities, or domains of each. While the governance meeting cannot decide pricing, it can decide which role is accountable for deciding, or which role controls the pricing model, or which other roles should be consulted before changing the pricing. For an organization to run smoothly, it's essential to clarify such matters. Without a strong focus a a clear space held for governance, it's easy to get so caught up in day-to-day operations that governance just doesn't happen, in which case the organization continues in its same old patterns. Regular governance meetings can change these patterns and dramatically enhance organizational clarity and agility.

GOVERNANCE RECORDS: YOUR ORGANIZATIONAL DNA

The organization's governance records describe its overall structure in detail and can be used to identify the expectations and authorities held by each role. Most people in an organization that is practicing Holacracy well will refer to these records regularly, even multiple times a day. The entire system will be undermined if the governance records are not clear and easy for everyone to access. You can use a generic wiki or similar intranet platform for this, if you configure it carefully, although a more structured tool is usually better. HolacracyOne offers a Web-based software platform called GlassFrog for this purpose (see glassfrog.com for more details). Even if you ultimately decide to use another tool for the job, a review of GlassFrog will help you understand what's needed in a good Holacracy support platform.

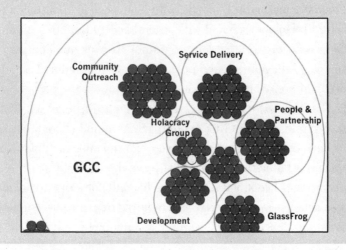

P 79 e

he Results of Governance

nce meeting process is useful for integrat-
ctives and driving clarity, what makes it
sformative is how the results shape day-to-day activ-
ity after the meeting. The roles and policies that come from governance form the keys to Holacracy's distributed power system and are the DNA of the organization's design—but all of this is lost if those involved don't fully understand what authority their roles convey. Fortunately, you can use this simple rule to remember the deeper meaning of role definitions and unlock the clarity encoded within:

> When you fill a role, you gain the **authority** to take any action you deem useful to express that role's **purpose** or energize one of its **accountabilities**, as well as you can with the resources available to you, as long as you don't violate the **domain** of another role.

Here's a tangible example of how this plays out: at one point, HolacracyOne's Outreach circle held a role affectionately named Social Media Butterfly, with a purpose to "pollinate the Web with Holacracy," and with several accountabilities, among which was "creating or sourcing quick-to-consume content of interest to our market, and posting it to social media channels and open-contribution websites."

That role was created in a governance meeting of our Outreach circle; the lead link of Outreach assigned Olivier, one of our partners, to fill the role. Olivier can thus use his judgment to define what actions would best serve the Butterfly's purpose or express its accountability, and he has full authority to execute those actions—with no approvals required from anyone—unless his actions "exert control" within the domain of another role.

Social Media Butterfly

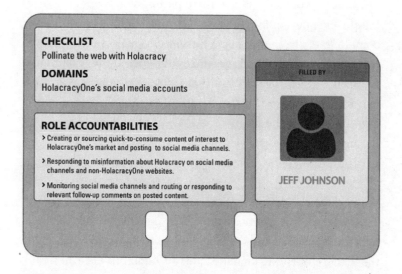

CHECKLIST
Pollinate the web with Holacracy

DOMAINS
HolacracyOne's social media accounts

FILLED BY

ROLE ACCOUNTABILITIES
> Creating or sourcing quick-to-consume content of interest to
HolacracyOne's market and posting to social media channels.

> Responding to misinformation about Holacracy on social media
channels and non-HolacracyOne websites.

> Monitoring social media channels and routing or responding to
relevant follow-up comments on posted content.

JEFF JOHNSON

So, for example, as our Social Media Butterfly, Olivier may freely decide to post comments on someone's blog relevant to Holacracy, but he wouldn't be able to, say, add our Facebook link to the slides for our certification training. That's because the domain of "certification training slides" was placed within our Program Design role in another governance meeting, and thus Olivier's authority in our Social Media Butterfly role is constrained—he can take that action only if he first gets the approval of Program Design. And on the flip side, the rest of our team can take actions they deem useful to express the purpose and accountabilities of their roles, but if they want to add something to our Facebook page they need Olivier's approval as Social Media Butterfly, because that role holds the domain of "HolacracyOne social media pages and accounts."

In this way, you can think of a domain as a property right, and that leads to another simple rule of thumb for practicing Holacracy: you are free to do whatever you wish with your own property (your role's domain), but not to exert control on your neighbors' property without their permission. We can extend this to include circles as well: if a circle has been granted a domain to control, and hasn't further delegated that domain to one of its roles, then that domain is considered the "communal property" of all roles within that circle, and any one of them can exert control within it. Think of the domain as a family car—anyone in the family can drive it at will, but the neighbor needs permission.

What Counts as a "Policy"?

The primary governance constructs that define how a circle works are its roles, and the elements we've discussed that define those roles: purpose, domains, and accountabilities. But there's another governance output worthy of definition: a policy. The Holacracy constitution gives the word a specific meaning that *excludes* what most people think of as "policies." In Holacracy, a "policy" is defined as "a grant or limit of authority to impact the domain of a circle/role." So when a circle controls a domain (its property), the circle may set a policy in a governance meeting either to allow outside roles to impact that property or to prevent its own roles from impacting that property in certain ways.

Let's take an example. One company I worked with, a content publishing company, included a Marketing circle with a domain of "the company website." That would normally prevent any roles outside that circle from impacting the website. However, the Marketing circle decided to adopt a policy, via governance, to allow certain outside roles to edit certain pieces of content. For example, a circle that hosted events was free to update event information on the website. The Marketing circle could also, if it saw fit, adopt a policy limiting how its own roles might impact the website; for example, a policy could prevent anyone from posting content without a sign-off from a Website Editor role. However, policies are not the right tool for most decisions apart from grants or limits of power to impact a domain. Policies should not be used to capture specific operational decisions, like setting prices, or to capture a general direction that people should head toward. In most cases these won't meet Holacracy's definition of a policy, and they're not valid outputs of a governance meeting. Also, be careful about policies that really should be captured as accountabilities; a policy can limit what certain roles may *choose* to do or how they may choose to do it, as in our example above, but if it sets an expectation that someone should *definitely* do something, then you want an accountability, not a policy.

Just as a circle defines policies in its governance meetings, so a role may define policies as well. This applies if the role has its own domain to control. For example, if the publishing company's Marketing circle puts a domain of "the company website" on its Website Director role, it is effectively delegating the authority to govern that domain from the whole circle to the Website Director specifically. The circle member filling the Website Director role would then have the power to create or modify policies to govern the website, outside of the circle's governance meetings (or rather, in his own governance meeting, of just one person). The circle may later undelegate that domain by removing it from Website Director, but until that happens, it's up to the Website Director role to control the website and define policies concerning who is allowed to impact it, and how.

The Rule of Individual Action

No matter how much organizational clarity we create through governance, situations will arise that require urgent response outside the normal bounds of a role's authority. What do you do when you are confronted by such a situation, with no time to consult with others, much less call a governance meeting? For example, I once found myself racing another company to register a key domain name for a website. My company at the time had a policy that all domain name acquisitions had to be done by our IT role, but this happened on a weekend; had I waited until Monday, I would have lost an important opportunity. More recently, I watched as a colleague jumped in and swapped room assignments during a company event, in a last-minute effort to make guests more comfortable, even though none of her roles had the authority to do so. She knew she was stepping on another role's toes, but she sensed a tension, couldn't get hold of the relevant role filler, and decided the room switch was the right thing to do to help the company.

For cases like these, the Holacracy constitution allows for "individual action"—effectively, there's a rule about how to break the rules. The individual action rule states that acting outside the bounds of your formal authority is allowed and shall not be considered a violation of the constitution, as long as: (1) you believe the action will resolve more tension for the organization than it might create; (2) there is no time to request any permissions normally required from other roles; and (3) the action does not commit the organization's resources or assets beyond what you are otherwise authorized to commit to. That's the summary version; you can find the full terms and details in the constitution.

This permission to act outside the rules comes with some corollary requirements. If you take individual action, you agree to inform other roles that may be affected and, on their request, to take further restorative action to resolve any tension created by your individual action. You also agree that if you repeatedly take the same individual action, either you will propose adding that action as an accountability to a role in a governance meeting, so that the pattern is appropriately encoded into the organization's structure, or you will find some other way to stop acting outside of the formal structure.

A Familiar Foundation

To put this all together, the Holacracy constitution brings two foundational elements of our broader human societies into our organizations: there's **rule of law,** through the defined governance process; and there are **property rights,** through clearly defined domains distributed across different roles. These features enable an interconnected autonomy that should be familiar from our day-to-day societal life, but there's a key distinction: while a domain grants *your role* a property right, it does not grant *you* a property right. Your responsibility, should you choose to accept a role in a Holacracy-powered organization, is that of a steward. You are controlling the role not for your own sake, but for its sake. Your job is to control its property and use its authority for the sake of its purpose—which, in turn, serves its circle's purpose, which ultimately serves the whole organization's purpose. Like the charge of a parent raising a child, your charge as role filler becomes a sacred duty, a stewarding of another's path in the world—an act of love and of service, not for your own sake, but nonetheless of your own free will.

OPERATIONS

Things won are done; joy's soul lies in the doing.

—WILLIAM SHAKESPEARE, *Troilus and Cressida*

Here's a piece of advice I picked up while working in the lean software-development world: "Slow down to speed up." Doing governance means slowing down. You pull back from the day-to-day work to improve the pattern of the organization, while taking time to integrate many perspectives and honor each. But you pull back in order to speed up operations, and that's precisely what good governance enables: getting the work done, day to day, much more effectively, efficiently, and productively. It grants you a clear understanding of your accountabilities and your authority, so that, knowing what is expected of you and what you can expect of others, you can better fill your roles. Good governance removes the waste we experience in conventional, top-down predict-and-control organizations, when countless hours get lost in confusion. And it allows workers to find their own intrinsic motivation and the autonomy and authority to act on it, liberating the potential of a truly empowered workforce to get stuff done.

With clear governance, you no longer have to wait for someone else to tell you what to do, or seek buy-in or consensus to get a project moving: you know what you are accountable for and whose input, if any, you need to get. Clear governance empowers you to use your own best judgment to energize your role and do your work. And whenever these factors are not as clear as you might like, you can use your judgment to temporarily fill in the gaps, and then go to the next governance meeting to generate more clarity with your team.

In Holacracy, the realm of operations is everything that happens outside of governance. Operations is about using the structure defined in governance to fill your roles and get stuff done. And it's about coordinating that work effectively with other team members, based on the role-ationships that governance has delineated. If getting your work done depends on someone else doing something, you can check the governance records to see what they are accountable for and thus what you have the right to expect of them. If you want to take an action and are unsure of whether you can do so, the governance records will tell you what authority you hold to act alone, and what constraints you need to honor. And when you do have the authority to act but worry that doing so may cause tension for others, it's much safer and more comfortable to just take action when you know any tensions that result will be transformed into organizational learning in the next governance meeting—and when your team had a voice in giving you that authority in the first place.

Within the foundational structure created through governance, Holacracy provides further operational distinctions, rules, and lightweight processes that help a team get work done together and express their roles. With some experience, this can enable a level of productivity that's quite remarkable. Alexis Gonzales-Black illustrated this nicely when I asked how her team's efforts were progressing at Zappos. She fills several roles within their Holacracy Facilitation circle, which has taken on the sizable project of training internal facilitators and helping launch over four hundred new circles during Zappos'

Holacracy rollout. Alexis told me that "the outputs of this circle are staggering, from scaling the number of certified facilitators from zero to sixty-three in less than eight months, to creating and implementing quality control programs and policies, to housing the departmental rollout leads who are on track to have the entire company working in Holacracy by the end of the year. The kicker? Most of the role fillers are only committing about 5 percent of their time to the work of this particular circle. The ability for people to pull together fractions of their time and accomplish something so big is really a testament to Holacracy."

We'll turn now to some of the core processes and rules that help enable this kind of productivity, as we further explore the realm of operations, Holacracy-style.

The Basics

If we want to get things done with minimal drag, it helps to understand clearly what outcomes we want to achieve and what next steps will get us there. The constitution defines a "project" as an outcome to achieve, and a "next-action" as a concrete, physical action that could be executed now, at least in the absence of competing priorities. For these definitions, I am indebted to David Allen, the author of *Getting Things Done*, who taught me much of what I know about effective individual organization and whose work was a key influence in Holacracy's development. As David explains, "You don't actually do a project; you can only do action steps related to it. When enough of the right action steps have been taken, some situation will have been created that matches your initial picture of the outcome closely enough that you can call it 'done.'"[11]

For example, I once had a very messy garage, and decided I'd take a next-action to "clean my garage." Yet whenever I had some free time when I could potentially have done something about my garage, I'd hit a psychic block—I'd just feel over-whelmed and turn my attention to anything but the garage. My problem was that "clean my garage" is not a next-action; it's an outcome I want to achieve that will take multiple concrete actions to complete. That is, it's a project. The project felt over-whelming because I hadn't done the thought work required to identify a concrete next-action to move it forward. I've often noticed how stubbornly the human mind resists getting that clarity until our conscious will forces it, and my willpower wasn't at its strongest while staring at my messy garage. As David warns, "Most people resist creating their projects list like the plague. The visionary folks have trouble nailing their Big Ideas down to a component that concrete. And the busy peo-ple don't like having to define what they're actually trying to accomplish with all their activity. Yet this is the most func-tional and important list to have, to keep from being over-whelmed by the nitty-gritty operational realities of your life."[12]

Once I actually captured "garage clean" as a project, I was free to uncover my real next-action; the thought process went something like this: "I've got lots of broken-down cardboard boxes in there that I want to recycle, but there are too many to leave at the curb, so I need to find a recycling center. I think my township has one somewhere, and I bet it's listed on their Web page." So my next-action was "Google recycling center to find hours of operation and address." Now that I had clearly differentiated my project from my next-action, I felt no tug to procrastinate; in fact, the action was something I could do eas-ily and that would give me the feeling of a quick win. And once it was done, I identified another next-action, and another, until at some point I had a pretty clean garage, without feeling over-whelmed on the way.

It helped to have the project identified separately from the next-actions, because I could check off an action without worrying about losing sight of my overall goal. And even beyond that, capturing removed both the subtle stress and the waste of mental energy from holding all of my needed work in my head, which would have detracted from my ability to be fully focused and present moment to moment. Maintaining separate lists of projects and actions liberates my mind for better things. As simple as that is, I can't tell you how many executives I meet who are needlessly overwhelmed—or at least less productive than they could be—in part because they are not distinguishing between projects and next-actions.

The Holacracy constitution introduces that basic distinction. To help sharpen it for new Holacracy practitioners, I recommend a specific format for capturing a project: *write it as a true-or-false statement that is false right now but will be true when the project is done.* This forces you to clarify what the actual outcome is, and helps everyone know what "done" looks like. For example, rather than having a project in your list named just "new website," you might capture it as "new website developed" or "new website launched," depending on what outcome you're actually going for. Rather than "customer training," try "all customers trained on new widgets." The former constructions allow more room for vagueness and lack of clarity. The latter invite a simple question: Is it true yet? If not, what's the next step to make it true?

PROJECTS VERSUS NEXT-ACTIONS

A project is "any desired outcome that requires more than one action step."

A next-action is "the next physical, visible activity that needs to be engaged in, in order to move the current reality towards completion."

Source: David Allen, *Getting Things Done.*

Individual Organization

Holacracy's authentic distribution of authority transforms the arena of operations by giving people throughout an organization clear autonomy to take decisive action. But with that authority comes increased accountability to self-manage. In fact, under the Holacracy constitution, someone who accepts a role assignment also takes on certain explicit responsibilities. These include:

- **Sensing and processing tensions** around the role's purpose and accountabilities, through the various channels available
- **Processing accountabilities:** regularly identifying specific next-actions you could take and defining projects you could work toward to fulfill the role's accountabilities
- **Processing projects:** regularly identifying next-actions that would move each of the role's projects forward
- **Tracking projects and next-actions:** capturing all of the role's projects and next-actions in a database or tangible form accessible to others, outside your own mind
- **Directing attention and resources:** consciously and continually choosing the next-action or other activity that it makes most sense to direct your attention and resources toward, all things considered, and then taking that action.

In order for any individual to fulfill these responsibilities, a good system for individual self-organization becomes a necessity—a lightweight, flexible practice that allows you to consciously choose the best action to take at any given time, among all options available to you. You won't meet that threshold if you go through your days with your head and inbox full of "stuff" that you know you need to do something about, but that isn't reliably translated into a practical inventory of everything you could do, in a system that lets you quickly and confidently choose among those tasks. Holacracy does not specify what organizational system individuals should use to meet the basic requirements above, just that they find a way to meet them—and doing so will require both a good system and new habits to go along with it.

Duties of a Circle Member

In addition to their basic responsibilities as role fillers, individuals also have specific duties to their fellow circle members. These include offering **transparency** about projects and workflow; **processing** requests, accountabilities, and projects when asked to do so by others in the circle; and accepting certain rules of **prioritization** for your time, attention, and other resources. You can find full details in the constitution, and a summary below.

Duty of Transparency
The duty of transparency is particularly important for team alignment. Each circle member is expected to provide transparency to other circle members, upon request, regarding

1. **Projects and next-actions:** sharing the projects and next-actions tracked for any of his or her roles in the circle.
2. **Relative priority:** sharing his or her judgment of the relative priority of any tracked projects or next-actions compared with other activities.
3. **Projections:** sharing a rough estimate of when he or she will likely complete a project or a next-action, given current information.

4. **Checklist items and metrics:** During tactical meetings, reporting on metrics requested by the lead link and on checklist items requested by other circle members. We will examine these further later in this chapter.

Duty of Processing

The duty of processing means that in addition to the duties you hold in your roles, you are also accountable for processing messages and requests from other circle members; specifically:

1. **Processing accountabilities and projects:** upon a request to process an accountability or a project, you have the duty to process it into a clear next-action, or to get clarity on what it's waiting for.
2. **Requests for projects and next-actions:** upon a request to take on a specific project or next-action, you have the duty to consider the request, and to take on the task if it fits one of your accountabilities.
3. **Requests to impact domain:** upon a fellow circle member's request to impact a domain you control, you have the duty to consider the request and, if you decline, to explain why the proposed action would cause harm.

Duty of Prioritization

The duty of prioritization constrains how you deploy your time, attention, and other resources, using the following rules.

1. **Processing over ad hoc execution:** you have a duty to prioritize processing inbound messages and requests from fellow circle members over performing next-actions for your own roles, except for certain time-constrained work. Note

that this duty only extends to *processing* the inbound messages into clear next steps, and not necessarily taking those next steps.

2. **Requested meetings over ad hoc execution:** when a fellow circle member requests you attend a governance or tactical meeting, that takes priority over getting work done (again, except for certain time-constrained work).

3. **Circle needs over individual goals:** you have a duty to prioritize in alignment with any priorities or "strategies" specified by the lead link of the circle—a topic we'll return to in a later chapter.

Tactical Meetings

As one of my business partners says, "With Holacracy, nothing gets in the way of the work"—a useful mantra when considering what *not* to bring to a meeting. If you know what you need to do next and nothing is in your way, *just go do it*. If you know whom you need to talk to in order to move a project forward, *just talk to them*. But if you're not sure what to do and want some help, or haven't had a chance to coordinate with the right people during a busy week, the weekly tactical meeting provides a fallback. Tactical meetings are fast-paced forums to synchronize team members for the week and triage any issues that are limiting forward progress. They enable you to discuss operational issues, get updates on projects that other roles are working on, give updates on your projects, and ask for help when needed.

After a check-in round, tactical meetings start with several steps designed to bring out information that provides a picture of the circle's current reality, including a review of checklist items and metrics, and a space to share project updates. I call this the preamble to the meeting. Then an agenda is built on the fly, consisting of specific tensions to address in the meeting. The circle proceeds through each item in turn, with the goal of finishing the entire list within the time allotted. Even moderately skilled circles using this meeting process are able to do so quite reliably and effectively.

TACTICAL MEETING PROCESS

1. Check-in Round

Goal: Notice what's got your attention, call it out, let it go.
Sacred space: no cross talk. Get present, here and now; grounds the meeting.

2. Checklist Review

Goal: Bring transparency to recurring actions.
Facilitator reads checklist of recurring actions by role; participants respond "check" or "no check" to each for the preceding period (e.g., the prior week).

3. Metrics Review

Goal: Build a picture of current reality.
Each role assigned a metric reports on it briefly, highlighting the latest data.

4. Progress Updates

Goal: Report updates to key projects of the circle.
The facilitator reads each project on the circle's project board and asks: "Any updates?" The project's owner either responds "no updates" or shares what has changed since the last meeting. Questions allowed, but no discussion.

5. Agenda Building

Goal: Build an agenda with placeholder headlines.
Build agenda of tensions to process; one or two words per item, no discussion.

6. Triage Issues

Goal: Get through all agenda items in the allotted time.
To resolve each agenda item:

1. Facilitator asks: "What do you need?"
2. Agenda item owner engages others as needed.
3. Capture any next-actions or projects requested and accepted.
4. Facilitator asks: "Did you get what you need?"

7. Closing Round

Goal: Harvest learning from the meeting.
Each person can share a closing reflection about the meeting; no discussion.

VISIBLE INFORMATION

Another key to effective operations in Holacracy is the creation of a shared space where current projects, checklists, and relevant metrics can be displayed and easily reviewed. We call this a visual management system. It could be a physical corkboard on a wall, or a virtual space, such as an intranet page, a shared spreadsheet, or a view in a Web app that provides project-tracking functionality.

Visible Information

CHECKLIST

- Back up Website & Database
  [**Website Manager**, Weekly]
- Pay Bills [**Finance**, Monthly]
- Email Mailing List [**Marketing**, Monthly]

METRICS

	MARCH	APRIL	MAY
WEBSITE HITS Website Manager	8,500	9,000	
WIDGETS PRODUCED Widget Production	912	943	
WIDGET DESIGN CHANGES Widget Design	7	6	
SUPPORT CASES HANDLED Customer Support	49	51	
REVENUE Finance	$180K	$150K	

PROJECTS

TAX RETURNS FILED & PAID
FINANCE

NEW CAMPAIGN LAUNCHED
MARKETING

NEW FAQ PUBLISHED
CUSTOMER SUPPORT

WIDGET DESIGNED FOR NEW MARKET
WIDGET DESIGN

NEW EQUIPMENT INSTALLED
WIDGET PRODUCTION

Let's walk through the process, as it might occur in a tactical meeting at the Better Widgets Company. After the **Check-in Round**, which uses the same format as a governance meeting, a tactical meeting goes to a **Checklist Review**. A checklist is a list of recurring actions team members intend to take regularly, and the purpose of this step is to provide visibility into whether each recurring action has been completed over the prior week, month, or other target frequency. Checklist items can be defined by a role filler for her own role, or by any other circle member requesting that the role filler add one of her recurring actions to her checklist. The checklist is a simple but powerful tool for confirming that these recurring actions have been taken each period—at least, any actions that someone asks to add to the checklist. In our example, the Marketing circle has a monthly checklist item: "send email newsletter to mailing list." The facilitator reads it off, and the Marketing lead link says "check," meaning it was completed for the prior month. The Website Manager role has a weekly checklist item: "back up website and database." The facilitator reads off the item; Website Manager says, "No check" and adds a brief explanation: "We're having issues with the Web backup system, which we're working with the provider to resolve." Another circle member comments, "We're always having issues with that system, maybe we should . . ." No open discussion is allowed at this point, so the facilitator quickly cuts him off, and instead invites him to raise an agenda item when the process reaches the Triage Issues step if he has something he'd like to discuss. This step is just for getting quick data, not for bringing up or processing tensions about that data.

Next comes a **Metrics Review,** in which team members quickly surface relevant data to build a picture of current reality. Metrics for each role to report are specified by the circle's lead link; some may be reported every week, while others may be designated as every month or every quarter. For Better Widgets' General Company circle, the monthly metrics include number of website hits, number of widgets sold, revenue, number of customers on active support agreements, and number of support cases handled. During this step, clarifying questions are allowed, so as to bring out more data about the metrics, but any discussion or action taking desired should be held and brought up as an agenda item during the Triage Issues step. For example, when Widget Sales gives the number of widgets sold, the Marketing lead link asks, "Were those sales a result of the email campaign we just did?" Widget Sales responds: "Yes, I think so." That's a fair question. But then Finance suggests that maybe we should consider doing a similar campaign every month—at which point the facilitator cuts him off and invites him to raise it during the Triage step if desired.

After metrics, the process moves on to **Progress Updates.** During this step, the facilitator reads aloud each project the team is tracking. Better Widget Company's projects include "New Blog Published," a project owned by Marketing; "New Super-Widget Designed," owned by Widget Design; and "New Customers Fully Trained on Widget Maintenance," owned by Customer Support. One at a time, the facilitator asks whoever owns each project, "Any updates?" The owner is then invited to share what has changed since the last tactical meeting—but not to give a general status report. I've noticed that when someone is asked for a general status report, the amount of actual progress is often inversely proportional to the amount of talk, because sharing a lot about the general status of your project is a great way to distract from lack of progress. So this step is specifically focused on what has *changed*. If nothing has changed with a project, the owner simply says, "No updates." The Marketing lead link says that the new blog is almost done now, and the rep link adds that the team just finished proofreading the first few posts and they should be live soon. Widget Design has no updates on the new super-widget design project. Customer Support explains that some of the new customers are on vacation and then begins elaborating on her training plans for them, but the facilitator soon cuts in and asks, "Does that mean there are no updates?" Customer Support concedes, "Yes, no updates, but we need a better system for scheduling their training sessions." The facilitator invites her to raise that during the Triage step. As with all of these "preamble" steps, the goal is just to draw out information; clarifying questions are allowed, to get more information out, but efforts to analyze or resolve anything are held for Triage.

With the preamble done, the team is now ready to **Triage Issues.** An agenda is built on the fly, with each agenda item owned by the person who raised it. Website Manager adds "backup service." Marketing lead link adds "email campaign." Customer Support adds "training prerequisites." In addition to any items like these that surface during the preamble, there are usually other items that people have noted for themselves in advance, which they'd like to raise in the meeting. Finance adds an item—"discounts." Marketing lead link adds another item: "website downtime." And Website Manager adds an item: "marketing descriptions." As in a governance meeting, an agenda item does not represent a general topic to discuss, but a specific tension to process. And the goal is not to resolve that tension for everyone, but just for the circle member who raised it—others can add their own agenda items if they have more to process.

Each agenda item is processed by giving its owner the space to engage others until their tension is addressed, or at least until one or more next-actions or projects are assigned that would move it forward. This driving focus enables tactical meetings to move quickly and efficiently. It starts with the facilitator asking the agenda item owner, "What do you need?" That person is then free to ask for help, while the facilitator listens for accepted next-actions or projects and asks the secretary to capture any that result.

We'll jump ahead to Customer Support's agenda item "training prerequisites" as we continue our simulated meeting. When the facilitator asks her what she needs, she explains, "We have a number of customers signed up for our advanced training on super-widget usage, but I've discovered that many haven't had the prerequisite basic training to be well prepared for this event." The facilitator asks, "What do you need?" "I need a way to get these folks up to speed before the upcoming training," she replies. "They're really good customers and now that they've signed up, I don't want to turn them away. And for the future, I need a better system for checking that participants meet the requirements before they can sign up for a training."

Widget Design responds to Customer Support's first need. "I can easily create a video that will condense some basic design information about our super-widgets—if they watched that, they should be more prepared for the advanced training." Customer Support nods vigorously, so the facilitator asks the secretary to capture that as a project for Widget Design: "Basic Super-Widget Design Video Published."

Customer Support's second need is more complex. Website Manager says that redesigning the online training sign-up system to include a requirements check is not something we have the resources to do at this point. "I think we'll need to rely on a manual check for now," he suggests, and Customer Support says she'd like Website Manager to start doing that. Website Manager looks concerned and opens his mouth to object, but the facilitator steps in before he has a chance, and directs a question to Customer Support: "Is that an activity you'd like Website Manager to do on an ongoing basis, at least for a while?" After Customer Support confirms, the facilitator continues:

"Then it sounds like you're looking for a new accountability—an ongoing activity that you can expect someone to enact. We can only add accountabilities in a governance meeting, so would you like to take on a next-action to bring a proposal to governance?" Customer Support nods, and an action is assigned to her to create a proposal for resolving this issue and bring it to the next governance meeting.

Website Manager then jumps in to say, "I'm not sure that accountability should be on the Website Manager role, but we can sort that out in governance, and I'm happy to help by doing it in the meantime until our next governance meeting." The facilitator asks Customer Support if she got what she needed, and she responds affirmatively. That means we're ready to move on to the next agenda item.

Marketing lead link owns the next agenda item, "website downtime." She explains: "Last week the website went down for maintenance right after we had launched our email campaign." The facilitator asks, "What do you need?" She replies: "I need the Website Manager to give me notice before taking down the website." The facilitator asks, "Is that something you're expecting from Website Manager?" and, after getting a quick yes, asks the secretary to pull up the governance records to see if there's currently an accountability for anything like that on the Website Manager role. The records show no such accountability, so the facilitator continues, "There's no account-ability for that, so you have no right to expect it; would you like the right to expect it?" After getting another affirmative response, the facilitator asks the secretary to capture an action for Marketing lead link to propose that accountability at the next governance meeting.

The governance meeting will give Marketing lead link an opportunity to resolve her issue permanently, but the facilitator senses that something is needed beforehand. "Aside from figuring out those expectations longer term, is there anything else you'd like tactically to help address your tension in the meantime?" Marketing lead link asks Website Manager to take on a next-action to send her a schedule of currently planned website maintenance. Website Manager agrees and the secretary records the action. "Do you have what you need?" asks the facilitator, getting a quick "Yep" in reply.

The next item is from Website Manager: "marketing descriptions." He's about to launch a page for a new type of widget just added to the company's lineup, but he has no descriptive copy. "What do you need?" asks the facilitator. "I need a couple of hundred words describing the widget and what makes it unique," he replies. Marketing rep link offers a solution: "I just wrote a new blog post focusing on that widget, so you can use some of that copy for the general widget page as well." Website Manager is satisfied, so Marketing rep link takes on a next-action to email the blog post, and the meeting continues.

This simulation shows a team that's relatively new to Holacracy; more seasoned team members will often catch themselves when their tensions point to governance issues such as defining new accountabilities, and focus on work that's appropriate for tactical. Either way, the process illustrated in the example allows for a fairly fast-paced and focused meeting, even for a new team. The emphasis on clear and simple output grounds tactical meetings and keeps them moving. And the one-tension-at-a-time approach, with the only goal being to satisfy the person who raised the agenda item, keeps the meeting on track. Speed and focus are further enhanced because governance issues are separated out from tactical needs. Under the Holacracy constitution, governance can be modified only via the governance process, so when tensions surface about general patterns at play, or when someone wants to set a new ongoing expectation, a good facilitator will always suggest that the interested party take a next-action to raise the matter in a governance meeting, where she or he can seek such deeper changes with confidence that the integrative process will address them effectively.

Tactical meetings, like governance meetings, are thus kept on track and within the rules of the Holacracy game by the elected facilitator. His or her role is to hold to the process; to keep the resolution focused on just the agenda owner's tension with tactical output; and to bring attention, when necessary, to the governance records and the expectations and authorities they grant. While processing an agenda item, a good facilitator will continually return to the agenda item owner to check, "Do you have what you need?" As soon as that person says yes, it's time to move on to the next item. If anyone has a new issue that's triggered by the discussion but that doesn't get addressed, that person can add an agenda item and get the same focus on his tension when it's his turn to process it.

Once the meeting is finished, the secretary shares the list of projects and next-actions captured with all circle members, either via email or by capturing them directly into a tool that automatically sends notifications.

TIPS FOR FACILITATING TACTICAL MEETING TRIAGE

If . . .

. . . analysis or discussion feels overdone
Ask: *"What next-actions are needed here?"*
Ask: *"So, what do you need?" (to agenda item owner)*

. . . people are seeking consensus or buy-in
Ask: *"What role has the authority to make a decision here?"*
Ask: *"Do we need to clarify authorities in governance?"*

. . . "leaders" are referenced by name
Ask: *"What role are you engaging here?"*

> **. . . a broader or recurring pattern needs to change**
> **Ask:** *"Is this a pattern to address in governance?"*
>
> **. . . someone is trying to set a new expectation**
> **Ask:** *"Is that something you'd like to expect on an ongoing basis?"*
> If so, *"Would you like an action to bring that to governance?"*

No More What-by-Whens

A final and important note on operations and getting stuff done: on a day-to-day level, Holacracy obsoletes the habit of making commitments about when you will deliver a particular project or action. In tactical meetings, for example, we capture next-actions, but do not attach deadline commitments to them. Why? As much as the practice of setting deadlines is generally recommended in today's business world, allow me to offer a contrary view: committing to deadlines has important downsides, and using them obscures a more dynamic, reality-based approach.

The alleged benefit of routinely asking for or offering a "what-by-when" upon defining actions is simple and straightforward: it increases others' confidence that we'll actually do it, encourages us to consciously own our commitments, and builds trust over time by showing others that we can uphold these commitments. Sounds great, and indeed it's vastly better than an environment where no one can count on anything, because everyone just works on whatever happens to catch his or her attention in any moment. So I'm not suggesting you throw out what-by-whens and move backward to chaos.

With Holacracy at play, accepting a next-action in one of your roles, in a tactical meeting or otherwise, is by definition making the commitment to (1) consciously track the action; (2) consciously review the action along with others you could take, as you continually assess where to direct your attention and energies; and (3) consciously do the action as soon as it becomes the most important item among your possible actions, all things considered. The selection of work according to date commitments is sometimes at odds with the constitution's requirements, and those trump any date commitment you might give: you might need to consciously and continually select a more valuable use of your attention and energy, and as a result miss a promised due date. The constitution sets a higher bar of conscious prioritization than just making quick date commitments and then driving your work by them; it allows you to use external deadlines as key data when prioritizing work, but it also requires your continual, conscious consideration, given the context and given everything else on your plate.

To put it another way, sometimes reality dashes our best-laid plans to rubble. And even when we do manage to temporarily control the wild whims of reality, the what-by-when approach still entails significant costs and risks. Let's say I'm in a meeting and agree to take an action. You ask me when I'll have it done by. I think for a second and say, "By Tuesday," which satisfies you, and thus we have a makeshift social contract. Here's the trouble: when I agreed to finish the action by Tuesday, I didn't actually create any more hours in a day to do it, as nice as that would be. So I've now got to fit this action into a list of other possible things I could be doing with those hours, and thus I have to de-prioritize something else.

That is, when I gave you a by-when commitment, I made a decision about priorities that affected the timing of many other actions—and I did it without looking at those actions, certainly without weighing the relative priorities of everything I'm accountable for. My conscious commitment came with unconscious prioritization. And there's more: I've also introduced the new risk that I will end up working on something so as to meet a commitment—often an artificial commitment—regardless of whether it's the most important thing for me to be working on in the moment, given the organization's broader purpose.

With by-whens flying around, it's easy to end up unconsciously chasing commitments rather than consciously selecting and working on the most important action in every moment. To give someone a by-when on an action doesn't make that action the most important thing to do; sometimes it makes sense to drop a task in the service of tackling a more important one that you hadn't anticipated when you made the original commitment.

Sure, you can manage that by resetting expectations, but that gives you another thing to manage and thus adds cost to giving a by-when commitment—the commitment adds rigidity and takes constant energy to hold. Yet another insidious cost is the weight of a looming deadline: it adds a psychic stressor, and tempts us to get stuck in our own "shoulds" and fight reality. Sometimes we try to conjure more hours in a day to deal with the stress of a by-when, but to subtract from our much-needed downtime can be quite taxing and in the long run is unsustainable.

The by-when approach helps us pretend that reality is more predictable and controllable than it actually is, a self-deception that's among the most comforting ones we humans engage in. And it's on this foundation that by-whens build trust—they lure others into the deception so they, too, can relax in a sense of certainty. It works, at least to a point, but that foundation is awfully shaky.

I'm not suggesting that we throw out what-by-when commitments without an effective replacement. But when we put in place an effective way of organizing our lives and our work—one that allows us to reliably hold everything we could do, and always be confident that we are working on the most important thing we could be doing in every given moment, fully consciously and without losing track of anything—we can let go of the illusion of control.

Once we've got good individual organizational systems in place that support consciousness and flow, we can now build trust by offering others transparency, grounded projections (not commitments), and a way to influence our priorities. Instead of offering our colleagues the illusion of predictability (often while we're barely holding it all together), we engage them in our process of relentlessly facing reality from moment to moment, and always working on the most important thing first.

So what about real external deadlines that you *do* need to plan around? The world is full of such deadlines, and Holacracy won't magically change the fact. But it will change how you manage working toward those deadlines and how you hold others accountable for their part in helping you meet them. Under Holacracy's rules, you can't hold someone accountable for a future date commitment even if they give you one, so meeting your own deadlines will require more ownership and involvement on your part. When you face time pressure, instead of asking for by-when commitments from others and hoping they meet them, you can instead ask about and influence the choices they're making while they work toward the outcomes you need, such as influencing how they prioritize actions you care about. And Holacracy provides many pathways for you to influence those choices and priorities; for instance, you can use the key duties described earlier in this chapter. The duty of transparency can help you get key information and monitor progress; the duty of processing might help you request certain key actions or projects; and the duty of prioritization means you can get a lead link involved in prioritization questions and expect others to align with the lead link's decisions.

Ultimately, these rules and Holacracy's other processes will help you take ownership and control of your own needs when a deadline is looming, and get involved with your colleagues early, as a partner, rather than late, as a judge. This shift illustrates a broader pattern in Holacracy as well: instead of holding people accountable for specific results, which can be affected by many things outside their control, Holacracy tends to hold people accountable for the choices they make while working toward those results, because our choices *are* within our control. Even beyond that, Holacracy gives you more ways to get involved early and influence those choices, before you ever need to hold someone accountable for making bad ones.

"Holacracy Wins!"

This combination of individual accountability, team transparency, and flexible, fast-paced tactical meetings helps to create efficient, adaptable, and productive operations. One of our clients recently shared a message he received after a Holacracy tactical meeting—it simply read, "33 agenda items in 55 minutes. #HolacracyWins!" I hear things like this from many Holacracy practitioners. People find they can get through agendas faster than they previously thought possible, with more real understanding and resolution than they used to get in a much slower process. If that doesn't happen for you, then you can always return to governance to process whatever tensions are getting in the way and slowing the work down, until you have the authority and freedom you need to get stuff done—fast.

6

FACILITATING GOVERNANCE

Seek freedom and become captive of your desires.
Seek discipline and find your liberty.

—FRANK HERBERT, *Chapterhouse: Dune*

Now that we've walked through the basics of the governance
meeting process with a simple example, and looked at how the
outputs of governance translate into day-to-day operations, it's
time to tackle some of the more complex dynamics that can
arise. We'll specifically examine how to deal with disruptive
behaviors by individuals in the circle, and how to test the validity of objections. We'll approach these issues from the point of
view of the facilitator, so that this section can serve both as
advanced instruction for facilitating governance meetings
and as a more detailed illustration of what governance is in a
Holacracy-powered company and how it works. The facilitator's
ability to effectively handle these more complex situations is
critical to a successful Holacracy practice, especially when
others are still learning to play the game. To build on our earlier analogy, the facilitator is like the referee in this new
sport—a neutral, impartial role designed to protect the process and uphold the rules of the game.

If you are already a skilled meeting or process facilitator

or coach, be warned: that experience is unlikely to have prepared you for this role; in fact, it usually gets in the way. A good facilitator within a conventional organizational power structure learns to be sensitive to all the people in a group, and to support and bring forward their different points of view—to help give them a voice. In a sense, the traditional facilitator becomes a heroic leader or parent figure for the duration of the meeting. The role of a facilitator in Holacracy is quite different—so different that it may feel counterintuitive. Your responsibility is not to support or take care of the people; it is to protect the *process*, which itself allows people to take care of themselves. The role of facilitator requires that you override your instinct to be polite or "nice" and that you cut people off if they speak out of turn—not just after they've aired their views, but even at their first intake of breath. Does that sound ruthless? It is, but for a reason. The process protects the ability of the proposer to address a tension, and it ensures that everyone else can keep problems from being created elsewhere as a result. Violating the process violates the proposer's space for addressing a tension safely, and it's the facilitator's job to ensure this doesn't happen. The rules may seem restrictive or overly rigid, but they yield liberating results—they create a sacred space that frees each of us to act as a sensor for the organization, without reactive drama getting in the way.

Done well, the process feels profoundly impersonal. As facilitator, you do not drive the meeting toward certain outcomes, but rather hold the space for the process itself to do its work. You don't try to invite input, and you don't try to get to agreement. As long as the process is honored, you really don't care how anyone feels—at least, not in your role as facilitator. You are neutral. When someone violates the process by talking out of turn, you simply stop the out-of-process behavior without emotion or judgment, and you do it immediately, without waiting for a comfortable pause. As far as you're concerned, the process is all that matters, and the process will take care of everything else. As I wrote earlier, your role is similar to that of a referee on the sports field—you serve the game, not the players. When you suppress out-of-process behavior, it's not because you're angry with the individual, any more than a referee is angry with a particular player when he calls a foul. He's simply protecting the game, and you are protecting the process.

Facilitating this impersonal process can be deeply transformative for all involved, and it holds the space to allow the organization's structure to continually evolve. Once people experience the power of this process, most find it difficult or impossible to go back to a more personal, consensus-driven approach. Yet learning to get there can be quite painful, as comfortable old habits must give way to challenging new ones. When I serve as an organization's Holacracy coach and initial facilitator, it's my job to hold a team to the new rules, even when—as isn't uncommon—some of the team members dislike them at first. That dislike may be turned on me, as the one holding the team to this strange new way of meeting and making decisions, and I occasionally become the target of ire. Fortunately, the anger is pretty short-lived; people who once scorned my presence may well be offering me hugs and gratitude a few months into an engagement, sometimes even with tears in their eyes. This reversal usually comes after they experience the impact of this new way of processing tensions and making decisions together, and realize how the new rules were critical to that transformation, even if adhering to them was initially uncomfortable.

What's Valid to Process?

To some extent, the "impersonal" quality of the Holacracy governance process arises from the types of tensions we're addressing in governance in the first place, and why we're addressing them. For a proposal to be valid to process in a governance meeting, the tension behind it must be somehow limiting one of the proposer's roles, and the goal must be to remove that limit, for the sake of the role. A proposal may *modify* other roles, as long as the *reason* is to help one of the proposer's roles—perhaps by making it easier to execute an accountability, or by harnessing an opportunity to better express the role's purpose. To enforce this restriction, a proposal can be discarded by the facilitator if, while processing the proposal, the proposer cannot give a concrete example of how the proposal would have improved his or her ability to express the purpose or accountabilities of one of his or her roles, given an actual situation faced in the past or present. One small exception is that you can also propose something to help another role you don't fill, as long as whoever actually fills that role has given you explicit advance permission to speak for it.

This rule will ultimately filter out two types of proposals that may seem desirable but that actually get in the way. The first are ungrounded or scattershot attempts to improve "everything," often including things that aren't the proposer's charge to improve in the first place. This tendency of certain idea-rich, helpful folks often distracts from getting work done by tinkering with and overdesigning governance that experience hasn't shown actually needs improvement yet. It's also sure to annoy those who work in the co-opted roles if they don't want the "help."

The second group of proposals this rule protects from are those that attempt to serve the proposer *personally*, not a role he is stewarding for the organization. For example, proposals about improving vacation policies, compensation systems, or travel policies may fall within this category—*unless* the proposer fills a role whose purpose or accountability is actually limited by them. Although, as in any relationship, it's important for us to figure out how to fulfill our personal needs, there are useful and appropriate boundaries here. If we want healthy relationships between the organization and its stewards, we don't want role fillers to co-opt the organization's space and internal processes just to meet their personal needs, any more than we want parents co-opting their children's lives and internal processes just to meet their own personal needs. The job of a role filler in a Holacracy-powered organization is to help parent the organization, not the other way around—we are stewards or fiduciaries for our roles and for the organization itself, and that obliges us to find a more appropriate way to address our personal needs, not to violate the organization's internal governance process with them. We might renegotiate an employment contract (or equivalent) with the relevant role to get certain agreements in place, or we might pitch a desired change to a role that's explicitly accountable for serving the organization's people somehow. There are many ways to get our personal needs met in our relationship with an organization, but governance is not one of them—it's about processing tensions for the sake of our roles, which ultimately serve the organization's purpose.

Facilitating the Mechanics

To take a deeper look at facilitating the mechanics of the governance process, let's return to the General Company circle (GCC) at Better Widgets. Imagine that you are now the elected facilitator for the circle. Even if you don't intend to ever play a facilitation role, stick with me, because understanding the basics of facilitation will make you a better Holacracy practitioner in any role, with a greater appreciation for the reasons behind the rules.

In the GCC governance meeting, you've completed a

check-in round, and you now invite circle members to add agenda items. At this stage you don't worry about whether proposals are valid; that usually becomes obvious during the clarifying questions phase or in integration. When building the agenda, assume all items are valid. Once the agenda building is complete, you are ready to begin processing tensions.

If there is one thing you as facilitator must remember when processing an agenda item, it's this: *one tension at a time.* Have you ever been in a meeting where one person raises an issue, and then everyone else jumps in trying to resolve their own tensions around that issue? Before you know it, you've got a tug-of-war match for the collective attention, with everyone trying to resolve his or her own issues, and a long painful meeting that actually resolves none very effectively. So stick with *one tension at a time.*

For this example, we'll focus on a particular tension that comes from the role of Widget Design. You enter the Integrative Decision-Making Process and start with the first step, "Present Proposal." The Widget Design role filler starts by explaining the tension: "Marketing keeps advertising with promises that our widgets are not designed to deliver on," he complains. Marketing lead link opens her mouth to respond, and you cut her off the moment you see that telltale intake of breath. This is not a moment for reactions or, indeed, for anyone other than Widget Design, who has raised the tension, to speak. You ask him whether he can make a proposal by finishing the sentence "I propose that . . . ," or whether he needs help crafting a proposal. Widget Design finishes your sentence by proposing that the Marketing circle's existing accountability for "promoting the company and its widgets" should be expanded to include "in alignment with the usage objectives defined for each type of widget."

Next, you invite clarifying questions. The Marketing lead

link jumps in immediately: "Have you considered exactly where those 'usage objectives' are going to come from? Those are never clear, and—" You quickly stop her again, because it's clear from her tone and her phrasing that this is not simply a clarifying question but rather a reaction in disguise. As facilitator, you must be ready for this common scenario. If the questioner sounds as if she is trying to convey a perspective of any sort to the proposer, you should cut her off and invite her to hold the thought until the reaction round. Whether she's offering a judgment or just a helpful piece of information, it counts as a reaction if she is seeking to convey perspectives *to* the proposer rather than to get perspectives *from* the proposer.

Another circle member then raises almost the same question, but from a genuine desire for clarification: "Where do you envision the usage objectives coming from?" This question is valid, but the proposer is not required to have or offer an answer; he can simply answer, "Not specified." Or he can provide an answer. In this case, he says, "We decide on them in our design meetings, and everyone is welcome to attend."

Now, with no further clarifying questions surfacing, it's time for the reaction round. You proceed around the participants, one at a time, inviting reactions. When her turn comes, your colleague in the Marketing lead link role is free to voice her reactions to the proposal, and she does. As facilitator, you don't care about reactions' content or tone, but you do make sure they are addressed to the space, and do not directly engage the proposer in an exchange. You also ensure that only one person speaks at a time and that each speaks in turn, and you allow no cross talk or response to reactions whatsoever. Don't get baited into stopping and debriefing about the dynamics in the group, or trying to defend any particular person or point of view. Hold your stance of total neutrality—simply let each person share her or his reaction, one at a time, and then move on.

Once all reactions have been voiced, it's time for the Amend and Clarify step, in which you ask the proposer whether he'd like to clarify anything or make any amendments to his proposal. At this point, proposers will often feel pressure to incorporate everything they just heard in order to honor their colleagues' perspectives. But that's not needed in this process; colleagues can raise their own agenda items if they want to process their tensions. So you make sure the proposer doesn't lose sight of his own tension: you help him focus just on that, inviting him to "be selfish" and ignore everything just said if it doesn't help with the specific tension he's trying to address, from his own perspective. He adds one clarifying comment with some background history that led to his proposal, and says he's happy with the proposal at this point, so no modifications to it are made.

Testing Objections

Next, you ask each person in turn, "Do you see any reasons why adopting this proposal would cause harm or move us backward?" That's the shorthand definition of an "objection." You invite each person to respond, simply, "Objection" or "No objection"—and, if the former, to say why adopting the proposal would cause harm or move the circle backward.

Once again, remember that what is being protected from "harm" is the circle's capacity to express its purpose and accountabilities, not the personal preferences and ideas of the circle members. So an objection needs to be related to a particular role the objector fills, and to describe how the proposal would diminish that role's capacity to express its purpose or enact its accountabilities. This keeps the organization from being overly influenced by individual feelings and opinions that are not relevant to the work of the objector. Facilitated well, the process helps people shift into a more impersonal space of organizational governance. The Reaction Round created an opportunity to acknowledge and honor whatever personal emotions were arising, but by the time you reach the Objection Round, the focus has shifted beyond those emotions. That having been said, you *can* use your emotions as clues to why a proposal may really cause harm for our roles. Personal emotions thus become sources of valuable information, but they aren't decision-making criteria in and of themselves. No one's voice is silenced, yet egos aren't allowed to dominate.

The objection process may sound simple, but it is not. This is a moment where your role as facilitator is critical, because it is your job to test the objections raised to discover whether they meet the criteria for validity. The Holacracy constitution provides four such criteria. We'll unpack each criterion through examples so you'll see how they work in practice.

A valid objection cites a new tension that would be created by adopting the proposal; *all* of the following must be true:

1. if the objection went unaddressed, the proposal would hurt the circle, not just fail to improve it (that is, it would diminish the circle's current capacity to express its purpose); *and*

2. the objection would be created specifically by adopting the proposal, and thus wouldn't exist if the proposal were dropped (that is, it is not a preexisting tension); *and*

3. the objection either arises from known data, or, if it's a prediction, there wouldn't be an opportunity to adapt before significant harm could be done (that is, it's not safe enough to try the proposal and just adapt later as needed); *and*

4. if the proposal had already been adopted, it would be valid for the objector to process the objection as a proposal (that is, the proposal limits one of the objector's roles)

Alternatively, the constitution also allows an objection that the proposal is unconstitutional (for example, "Not valid governance output"), even if the objection doesn't meet the

Testing Objections

An objection is valid if . . .

A) The proposal would degrade the circle's capacity.

| Is that a reason this causes harm or moves us backward? (and how?) | or | Is it a better idea or something else we should consider as well? | |

B) The proposal, if adopted, would introduce a new tension.

| Would that issue be created by adopting this proposal? (and how?) | or | Is it already an issue, even if we don't adopt this proposal? | |

C) The objection is either based on already known data, or, if it's a prediction, there wouldn't be an opportunity to adapt before significant harm could be done.

| Is that based on presently known data? | or | Are you anticipating that it might happen? |

| If anticipated: is there a reason we can't adapt once we get more data? | or | Is it safe enough to try, knowing we can revisit it anytime? | |

D) The objection would be a valid tension for your role to process.

| Does it limit one of your roles? (which one?) | or | Are you trying to help another role or the circle? | |

Valid Objection

OR if . . . E) The proposal breaks the rules of the Holacracy constitution:

e.g., "Not valid governance output," "Outside the circle's authority"

four criteria. Aside from that special case, you test objections against the criteria simply by asking questions. This process takes a while to get used to, but once you grasp the criteria more deeply, it will start to come quite naturally and you'll know intuitively what to ask to test objections. In the meantime, simply read off the questions one by one from the box on the previous page when an objection surfaces. It may seem silly, but it works quite well, and it will help the entire team learn.

For now, let's continue our example to see how testing objections might happen during an objection round. The proposal on the table is to expand the Marketing circle's existing accountability for "promoting the company and its widgets" to include the requirement that promotion be "in alignment with the usage objectives defined for each type of widget." The first objection is raised by the Website Manager: "The promotional content Marketing writes has been great for our print ads, but it's the wrong style and length for use on our website, so we also need Marketing to align with the style needs for Web content." This objection could be tested against criterion A above. As facilitator, you could ask: "Is that a reason that *this* proposal on the table now will cause harm or move us backward, or are you sensing another thing that we really need to fix as well?" Note the way this question is phrased—by giving the objector an either/or option, you help him distinguish between an objection and a separate tension. If you had simply asked the first part of the question, you would likely have gotten a simple yes, which would not help either party discern the validity of the claimed objection. But given both options, the Website Manager answers, "The latter," and has thus just told you that his objection isn't valid, because it's not a reason why adopting this proposal would cause harm or move the circle backward. You explain this to him, and instead invite him to add his tension to the agenda if he would like to process it separately. (A new agenda item can be added as soon as the current one is complete.)

In some cases, that question may not dissolve the objection: there may be a reason why the proposal would cause harm. Perhaps the Website Manager says, "Yes, it would cause harm, because there's already a big backlog of content I can't use for the website, and this would add to it." If so, you could try another test question to test against criterion B above— perhaps "So, if this proposal were withdrawn entirely and not adopted, would you still feel the tension that you are raising as an objection?" If the objector says, "Oh, yes, I'd definitely still feel it!," then he has revealed to you that the objection is not valid, because no *new* tension would be specifically created by this proposal. Rather, a separate tension already exists in the system. It may be perfectly valid as a separate agenda item, but it is not valid as an objection to the proposal on the table right now. At least with regard to this potential issue, adopting the proposal would not move us *backward*, it would simply fail to move us *forward* in addressing that issue too. But the only tension we're trying to address to move forward is the proposer's— nothing more.

The next objection sounds reasonable: "Marketing might not understand the usage objectives well enough to convey them effectively." However, once again there is a clue hidden in the language—in this case, the word "might." That indicates to you as facilitator that the objection may be predictive rather than based on present knowledge. You need to test it against criterion C above, so you ask: "Is that based on already-known data, or are you anticipating that it might happen?" The objector tells you she's anticipating it, which may be okay, so you ask a follow-up question: "Is there a reason we can't adapt later once we get more data, or is it safe enough to try, knowing we can revisit it anytime?" Sure enough, the objector tells you that it is safe enough to try, and has thus shown that this objection does not meet the threshold for validity.

Another suspect objection follows, raised by the always helpful lead link of the Widget Production circle: "Objection. I'm concerned that Marketing deals with so many different demands already that this will just be too impractical for them to manage." You test this one against criterion D: "Would the proposal limit or constrain one of your roles, or are you trying to help another role or the circle overall?" The lead link admits that it's not a concern for his roles; he's just trying to be helpful. So he's just told you that it's not a valid objection—although it might have been if someone representing Marketing had raised it, and if it met the other criteria.

These examples demonstrate how to use the criteria to test objections through questioning. Let's continue the objection round.

Someone says, "I don't think this is needed; the marketing descriptions are fine already." This objection does not meet criterion A—the objector may not think the change necessary, but if she cannot cite some harm that would result from the proposal, her opinion is irrelevant. Besides, the proposal makes no statement about whether the descriptions are fine or not at present; it simply sets an ongoing expectation about aligning with usage objectives.

Apart from not meeting the criteria above, an objection may also be invalid if it's based on a misunderstanding of Holacracy's rules and thus of what's actually being proposed. Suppose the Marketing rep link voices this objection: "We just don't have the resources to do it." The objection contains a clue to its invalidity: the word "resources." You're in a governance meeting, and governance decisions do not and cannot allocate resources. Adding an accountability only adds an expectation that the role filler (or, in this case, the sub-circle) define projects or actions that could be done to enact the activity, and then consciously decide how to divide whatever time and resources they do have across their many potential projects and actions.

To put it another way, you could execute an accountability for "aligning marketing with usage objectives" by taking a sixty-second action to copy and paste those objectives directly into the marketing material, or by a sixty-minute process of reviewing and editing them, or by spending six months and millions of dollars to hire McKinsey to do a thorough study of the matter; whichever route you take, you're enacting the same accountability. In governance, *you're allocating consciousness, not resources*—you are defining where the work lives, and who will figure out what portion of her available resources to spend on it, given everything else competing for those resources. You dissolve Marketing rep link's objection simply by explaining this fact, and then asking again whether he sees any reason the proposal would cause harm or move the circle backward, knowing that it doesn't actually allocate any resources.

With that possible objection dissolved, the Marketing lead link offers another: "Objection: I never understand exactly what the usage objectives are or who I can count on to define them." This one seems valid on all counts; if you're not sure, test it with a few questions like those above—if it's valid, it will stand up to the test.

Ultimately this objection does prove valid, so on the whiteboard you add it to the list of objections to resolve, but you don't do anything about it just yet—not until all circle members have had a chance to raise objections and the round is complete. Next up is Widget Sales, who says, "Objection: this won't address the tension, as there are other factors causing this problem."

However, you are only trying to resolve the tension from the proposer's perspective, so whether anyone else thinks it will be resolved is irrelevant. If they still feel tensions they want to resolve, they can add their own agenda items. So you ask, "Do you see a reason adopting this proposal would actually cause harm, or do you just think it won't address the tension?" The answer is the latter, and thus you've been told the objection is not valid—it isn't a reason adopting the proposal will cause harm.

You continue the objection round until all objections have been raised and tested. Remember, as facilitator, you're to hold the process of testing objections lightly. Your role is not to draw conclusions about the validity of the arguments raised, but simply to test potential objections with an attitude of scientific curiosity, until the validity or lack thereof becomes clear. You want the objector to tell you whether the objection is valid. If someone can give a specific, reasoned argument *why* the objection meets each specific criterion, then the constitution considers it valid, whether you agree with the arguments or not. As facilitator, you only judge *whether* a specific, reasoned argument has indeed been offered in support of each criterion; you do not have the authority to judge the *validity* of these arguments.

Once all objections have been voiced and tested, you are ready to integrate the valid objections that remain into an amended proposal.

Integration

In this example, one objection has emerged as valid and been charted on the board: "It's unclear what the usage objectives are or who will define them." You start by focusing the group on that objection, and asking, "What could we add to or amend in the proposal to dissolve that objection, while still addressing the original tension?" No one immediately offers an idea, so you specifically direct the question to the objector in the Marketing lead link role to get the search started, as the objector has a duty to at least try to find a possible integration. "Well, we can clarify whose job it is to define those usage objectives," she replies. Someone else adds, "They should come from Widget Design, and be published internally for anyone who needs them."

That sounds like an accountability that could be defined, so you turn to Marketing lead link and ask, "If we added an accountability to Widget Design for 'defining and publishing usage objectives for each type of widget,' so that you knew you could expect that from Widget Design, would that resolve your objection?" The response is a quick yes, so you check with the proposer, "And will the modified proposal with this addition still address your original tension?" Again you get a yes, so you check off the objection and ensure the secretary has captured the amended proposal, now with two parts—the expanded accountability on Marketing and a new accountability on Widget Design. With all the objections checked off, it's time to stop integration and move on. Whenever you complete the integration phase, you always go back to the objection round to test the modified proposal and see whether any new objections surface. Once you get through an objection round with no objections raised, the proposal is adopted.

The Power of Integrating Perspectives

As we saw in this example, Holacracy's governance meetings allow all the members of a team to use their perspectives to make proposals and raise objections, with confidence that their tensions will be integrated and resolved. This helps the organization avoid "outvoting the low-voltage light," because it only takes a lone human acting as sensor to resolve a key tension or prevent harm from someone else's proposal. However, this is not a consensus-based process. Only one person needs to sense a tension for it to be treated as relevant, even if no one else senses it and there's no "consensus" about it. Also, when seeking to resolve a tension, you are not looking for agreement or buy-in from the people personally, just data from the perspective of the roles they fill, and only about whether the proposal would cause harm or move the circle backward (reduce its capacity to express its purpose). A process that requires consensus is antithetical to one that seeks to process every tension and be truly integrative; it's also a recipe for letting ego, fear, or groupthink hinder the organization's purpose.

Yet even with a fast integrative process, most decisions faced in the course of day-to-day work are relatively simple and pose minimal risk. It would be a crippling waste of time to use this process for all of them, so Integrative Decision Making is used only in the foundational domain of governance, and not to make operational decisions (unless explicitly required by a governance decision). Thus, the integrative process in Holacracy is used to define space for autocratic control in specific areas, along with appropriate boundaries on that control. For example, a circle in charge of a product line could use the Integrative Decision-Making Process to define a role that handles all pricing-related analysis and decisions for its products. It might assign an accountability to the role for "defining pricing models for its products," and thus it would grant whomever fills the role the authority to perform that task. However, the circle might also define a limit or additional expectation along with this authority—for example, it might also require the role filler to align pricing with target-consumer profiles that are defined by another role, or to get Finance's assessment that a desired pricing model is expected to be profitable. Such constraints could take the form of additional accountabilities or of extra text tacked onto the one accountability for defining pricing. Or they could be captured as a separate policy.

With roles, accountabilities, and authorities defined concretely using an integrative process, the circle empowers its members to get the circle's work done and make specific decisions in service of that work outside of a governance meeting. At the same time, all circle members can fall back on the Integrative Decision-Making Process to further refine these grants and limits of authority, as tensions naturally arise during the course of work. The structure and rules of the process ensure that these tensions are channeled toward achieving the circle's purpose, and that destructive behavior is given no space and has no impact.

On a human level, regular governance meetings can transform the emotional tone of a team. Unclear governance leaves everyone with implicit expectations of who should be doing what and how they should be doing it. Without a defined governance process, it's easy to make up negative stories about others or toss around blame when unspoken assumptions clash—or to avoid those problems by pressuring people to align with implicit expectations, often through political cajoling or consensus building. Once governance meetings are introduced, team members have a forum for channeling the frustration of misaligned expectations into organizational learning and continual improvement, and they have available a more effective process for defining the shared norms any working team needs. Playing politics loses its utility, and personal drama gives way to a more authentic discussion of how to consciously evolve the organization in light of its goals and broader purpose in the world.

STRATEGY AND DYNAMIC
CONTROL

> When the number of factors coming into play in
> a phenomenological complex is too large, scien-
> tific method in most cases fails us. One need only
> think of the weather, in which case prediction
> even for a few days ahead is impossible.
>
> —ALBERT EINSTEIN, *Ideas and Opinions*

The operational paradigm I have been describing relies heav-
ily on individuals to manage and prioritize their own tasks and
responsibilities. But how do we ensure that there is also alignment within a team, to say nothing of a larger organization? In
a Holacracy-powered organization, where authority is genuinely
distributed and there is no ultimate heroic leader, it is critical
that we have ways to align our activities not just with each other,
but with what's needed now to express the organization's purpose. Tactical meetings certainly help, but there's another key
element to guide our decision making and help us all pull in
the same direction: a strategy. A good strategy helps us make
better day-to-day choices in what we prioritize and the paths
we choose operationally.

Inherent in this idea of strategy is a focus on the future.
But whenever we attempt to engage with the future, we find

ourselves on dangerous ground. Too often, corporate strategy is built on the misguided notion that we can reliably predict the future. Nassim Nicholas Taleb, one of the most cogent writers on the illusion of predictability, has said, "We cannot truly plan, because we do not understand the future—but this is not necessarily bad news. We could plan while bearing in mind such limitations. It just takes guts."[13] Eric Beinhocker makes a similar point: "Corporate leaders are expected to be bold generals who forecast the future, devise grand strategies, lead their troops into glorious battle—and then are fired at the first lost skirmish. It takes a courageous executive to push back against this mind-set, admit the inherent uncertainty of the future, and emphasize learning and adapting over predicting and planning."[14]

As Taleb and Beinhocker point out, in most conventional organizational contexts, strategy is the very essence of the predict-and-control mind-set—in setting strategy, we decide the right goals and then lay out a path for getting there. That whole approach is based on a fallacy. While there are some things we may be able to predict, there are many more that we simply cannot. We can't know the future state of the economy, or of our particular industry, and we can't foresee what innovations will disrupt the market or what opportunities may arise; in fact, it'd be easier to make the very short list of what we can reliably predict than to point out everything we can't, yet often try to anyway.

When we attempt to predict the future in an unpredictable world, not only are we deluding ourselves, but worse we are actually inhibiting our ability to sense and respond to reality in the present moment. When you impose a "should"—as in "I should be X in five years' time"—you create an attachment to that outcome; the attachment limits your ability to sense when reality is not going in that direction, or when other possible opportunities arise that might conflict with what you first set out to achieve. To illustrate this predicament, let's take one of my favorite metaphors, which I got many years ago from my work with agile software development methods. This metaphor should help illustrate the paradigmatic difference between conventional strategy and Holacracy's approach, before we get into the nuts and bolts of what the Holacracy constitution defines as a "strategy" and how to work with one.

Imagine riding a bicycle the way we manage most modern organizations. You would hold a big meeting to decide the angle at which you should hold the handlebars; you'd map your journey in as much detail as possible, factoring in all known obstacles and the exact timing and degree to which you would need to adjust your course to avoid these. Then you would get on the bicycle, hold the handlebars rigidly at the angle calculated, close your eyes, and steer according to plan. Odds are you would not reach your target, even if you did manage to keep the bicycle upright for the entire trip. When the bicycle falls over, you might ask: "Why didn't we get this right the first time?" And maybe: "Who screwed up?"

That ridiculous approach isn't so far from the approach many organizations take to strategic planning. By contrast, Holacracy helps an organization operate more like the way we actually ride a bicycle, using a dynamic steering paradigm. Dynamic steering means constant adjustment in light of real feedback, which makes for a more organic and emergent path. If you watch even the most skilled cyclist, you'll see a slight but constant weaving, as the rider constantly takes in sensory feedback about his present state and environment, and makes minor corrections to direction, speed, balance, and aerodynamics. Weaving arises because the rider maintains a dynamic equilibrium while moving forward, using rapid feedback to stay within the many constraints of the environment and equipment. Instead of wasting a lot of time and energy predicting exactly the "right" path in advance, he instead holds his purpose in mind, stays present in the moment, and finds the most natural way forward as he goes. That's not to say the rider doesn't have a plan or at least some sense of his likely route, just that he gains more control, not less, by surrendering to present reality continuously and trusting his capacity to sense and respond in the moment. Similarly, we have the opportunity to get more control in our organizations by more relentlessly facing reality and adapting continuously.

When we become attached to a specific predicted outcome, there's a risk we will get stuck fighting reality when it doesn't conform to our prediction. If we find that we are not on the path we set out for ourselves, we may conclude, sometimes subconsciously, that something must be wrong. That judgment of reality then inhibits our ability to respond, and encourages us to push against the unwelcome truth—to try to force reality to conform to our predicted vision. That's not a very effective strategy for navigating the ever-changing complexity of business today. When reality conflicts with our best-laid plans, reality usually wins.

I should note that embracing a more dynamic approach for gaining control is not at all the same as just "not predicting," any more than riding a bicycle is a process of "not steering." It's about changing how we relate to our predictions and plans, seeing them as sometimes useful fallacies, but not the primary tools to control the organization. And it's about being fully present in the here and now, so we can steer continuously in response to actual reality. When dynamic steering is done well, it enables the organization and those within it to stay present and act decisively on whatever arises day to day, like a skilled martial artist or the stereotypical Zen master.

Holacracy already encodes a more dynamic control process into its basic rules and processes. You may have noticed that in the governance and tactical meeting process, the focus is always on quickly reaching a *workable* decision and then letting reality inform the next step, rather than agonizing about what might happen in an effort to conjure up a theoretical best decision that still doesn't quite get it right. A ground rule of Holacracy governance is that any decision can be revisited at any time. This frees teams to move swiftly from discussion and planning to actually testing decisions in reality and learning from the results. Structure that starts out imperfect can quickly become well aligned with actual needs through a continual process of facing reality and incorporating feedback. The same can be said for many projects and other operational matters as well.

If you want to do conventional strategic planning despite these warnings, the Holacracy constitution certainly doesn't prohibit it—but under Holacracy's rules and processes, you will find it very difficult to drive others' behaviors on the basis of targets defined in advance. There are no rules requiring anyone to predict or control the future. However, the constitution does offer some alternative tools that can be used for more dynamic strategic alignment and prioritization across a team. We'll examine these next.

Strategy in Holacracy

We may not be able to map the perfect route to the ideal future, but we can often ascertain some orienting principles for navigation. Without trying to predict exactly what forks in that road we will encounter, we can ask ourselves what will help us to make the best decisions when we do come to a fork. When we step back to look at the broader context and the general terrain and options in front of us, we can often come up with guidelines, such as "Generally head east," or "Choose the easy roads even over the most direct roads." A rule of thumb like this really helps when we're confronted with a choice and want to benefit from wisdom generated when we had the luxury of pulling back and analyzing the bigger-picture context. When we distill that wisdom into memorable guidelines, we can apply them more easily and more regularly amidst the hustle and bustle of day-to-day execution.

This, then, is the form that strategy takes in Holacracy—an easy-to-remember rule of thumb that aids moment-to-moment decision making and prioritization (the technical term for such a rule is "heuristic"). I've found it useful to express these decision-support rules in the form of a simple phrase such as "Emphasize X, even over Y," in which X is one potentially valuable activity, emphasis, focus, or goal, and Y is another potentially valuable activity, emphasis, focus, or goal. Now, to make that useful, you can't just have X be good and Y be bad. "Emphasize customer service, even over pissing off customers" is not helpful advice. Both X and Y need to be positives, so that the strategy gives you some sense of which one to privilege, for now, given your current context. For example, one of HolacracyOne's strategies earlier in our company's development was "Emphasize documenting and aligning to standards, even over developing and co-creating novelty." Notice that both of those activities are positive things for an organization to be engaging in, but they are also polarities, in tension with each other. Our strategy is not a general, universal statement of value—in fact, if we tried to apply it forever it would undoubtedly cause serious harm eventually. There are times when it is essential to emphasize developing and co-creating novelty over documenting and aligning to standards. But for HolacracyOne, given our context at the time, and the recent history before that, and the purpose we're serving, that was our best sense of what to privilege, at least for a while: standardization, even at the expense of pursuing new and exciting opportunities.

Of course, no one was against the creation of novelty—for me, it often feels like the most natural way to operate. For the first few years of our growth, every event or training we did was unique and special, co-created on the fly with various partners who offered to host us and help market. This helped us to explore the new landscapes we were moving into, and it generated a lot of movement and some important relationships. But soon, our penchant for creating new and exciting offerings became unsustainable for that particular phase in our growth. It's expensive when every new offering is a custom product and each partnership requires hammering out a unique deal. We arrived at the strategy I've cited so as to redress the balance, to stabilize the organization and make it more efficient and sustainable. It provided useful guidance and had a focusing effect as we navigated the daily decisions we each faced. And ultimately, the strategy became irrelevant—we had integrated these two poles pretty well and found the harmony between them, and it was time to focus elsewhere.

As an example of how the standardization-first strategy helped: in my Program Design role in our Holacracy Education circle, from time to time I'd get an email from someone who had heard about Holacracy, gotten inspired, and now wanted to partner to create a new type of event for his particular business sector. I get excited by opportunities like that, but our strategy reminded me that at that moment in our development, I should instead invest my time and energy in standardizing our existing programs and events—even if it meant missing this new opportunity.

The standardization-first strategy helped our Customer Relations role when a question came in that she had never answered before. Rather than firing off a quick email in answer and moving on, she would take the time to create a standardized response and document it, or perhaps add it to our website's FAQs, so that next time a similar question was asked she didn't have to start from scratch.

PREDICTION VERSUS PROJECTION

While Holacracy's approach to strategy resists relying on predictions, that's not to say all forward-looking projections and anticipatory thinking are useless. In this regard, it's helpful to understand the difference between a prediction and a projection. "Predict" comes from the Latin *præ-*, "before," and *dicere,* "to say"—thus it literally means "to say before," or "to foretell, prophesize." "Project," on the other hand, is from the Latin *pro-*, "forward," and *jacere,* "to throw"—thus, "to throw forth." In order to throw forth, you must be firmly grounded in the place you are starting from: the present reality. Getting real data and "throwing it forth" to get a sense of where events are headed is often useful to better understand your context, and it is different than "foretelling and prophesizing" where reality will be in the future.

Strategy Meetings

The Holacracy constitution requires that individuals align their operational decisions with any strategies specified by a circle's lead link, and it's left up to each lead link to decide what process to use to figure out useful strategies. In some circumstances, it may be sufficient and advisable for the lead link to simply use his or her individual judgment and set a strategy. Of course, this risks missing other important perspectives or useful insights, and it certainly fails to tap the collective wisdom of everyone working in the circle day to day. A lead link may wish to use a brainstorming process of some sort to collect input before declaring a strategy, or even a more structured group process designed specifically for defining Holacracy-style strategies. Some circles and organizations I've worked with have adopted a policy to require such a process, by constraining the lead link's authority to set a strategy autocratically.

Although the constitution specifies no single process for defining strategies, we've experimented with various processes over the years in my organization and helped our clients do the same. As a result, we've come up with a generic "strategy meeting" process that works pretty well for most circles I've experienced, and I think it's a good option to consider for a lead link looking for an effective way to define strategies with input. A strategy meeting is typically held in each circle about once every six months, and it generally takes about four hours, or perhaps five or six. The goal of these meetings is to map the circle's recent history and current context to orient everyone, and then to identify strategies to help the team steer into the future. Where conventional strategic planning processes typically look for a specific plan, these meetings seek merely to find good rules of thumb for decision support. Rather than mapping a specific "right course," they're about equipping the team with the right compass to guide them along the journey.

Following is an overview of the process.

STRATEGY MEETING PROCESS

1. **Check-in Round**
2. **Orientation:** Review purpose, domain, and accountabilities of circle, and any strategies of super-circle.
3. **Retrospective:**
   - Each participant silently reflects and captures notable facts, data, events, and history.
   - Participants post their notes on the wall, and collectively organize/group related ones.

- Participants describe/clarify key notes and share reflections; facilitator makes a list of key tensions raised while sharing.

4. Strategy Generation:
- Capture and post ideas individually: what should we emphasize, given these tensions?
- Discuss collectively: what strategy or strategies should guide us, looking forward?
- Lead link proposes one or more strategies; these are processed via Integrative Decision Making.

5. Unpack the Strategy
- Each participant individually reflects and captures projects and next-actions to take in his or her role.
- One at a time, each participant shares what he or she has captured and solicits/receives input and ideas.

6. Closing Round

1. Check-in Round

Like governance and tactical meetings, strategy meetings begin with a check-in round.

2. Orientation

Once the check-in round is complete, the facilitator highlights the purpose, domains, and accountabilities of the circle, plus any strategies defined by the circle's super-circle. This brief orientation serves to focus everyone on the identity of the circle and what it's trying to achieve, plus its context and any relevant strategies.

3. Retrospective

The purpose of the retrospective is to reflect on how you arrived at the present moment and what the current landscape looks like. Capture and post relevant points, and don't judge the emerging picture or discuss what to do about it here, just bring things up and capture them until you have a robust picture of your current context. I've found an effective way to facilitate this step is to hand out pads of very large sticky notes, and have team members write their points on these, one per sticky note, in big letters. Participants post their notes on a wall for all to see, and then group and organize them in natural clusters of related points. Once the stickies are grouped, the facilitator asks for comments, clarifications, or reflections about the notes within each cluster, one at a time, and records any tensions expressed in the process.

4. Strategy Generation

The next step is for each individual to reflect on the question "What might make sense to emphasize day to day to help address these tensions?," and to make note of any ideas she or he has. Notice that you are not asking how to address the tensions with specific actions or projects or new governance. You're asking for a general emphasis, a rule of thumb to apply. Two or three ideas per person is typical, posted on large sticky notes just as in the previous step. When we established Holacracy-One's early strategy, it became clear when these notes were first posted that we needed to emphasize standardization in some way, because a number of the suggestions mentioned it in one form or another.

Once the suggestions are posted, a more convergent discussion starts, to hash out the specific strategy: "What should we emphasize? What strategy should guide our decision making?" At this point, remember the format I recommended for strategies: "Emphasize X, *even over* Y." The *"even over* Y" part of the equation is quite powerful—without it, just emphasizing one particular thing won't be as meaningful or helpful. "Documenting and aligning to standards" doesn't give us much to work with until it is juxtaposed with "over developing and cocreating novelty." With the explicit articulation of the polarity, suddenly we have a powerful decision-making aid.

As another example, one circle we worked with wanted to change the way they went about sales and marketing, so they defined a strategy of "authentically attract, *even over* chasing"— the first part alone might have been a nice reminder, but the second made a much stronger statement about changing priorities.

Once the discussion has come to a natural alignment and conclusion—or when the lead link believes it's close enough that it's not worth time or energy to improve the exact wording further—then the lead link cuts off discussion and proposes one or more specific strategies. That proposal is processed using the Integrative Decision-Making Process (see p. 72), as in governance meetings.

5. Unpack the Strategy

Once the new strategy or strategies are established, each individual takes a few moments to consider, "What could I do in my roles to better enact the new strategy?," and to record any ideas that result. Once everyone has had a chance to reflect, participants share their ideas, one person at a time, and others may offer input and further suggestions. This typically results in many new projects and actions, plus some agenda items to bring to the next governance meeting.

6. Closing Round

Like governance and tactical meetings, strategy meetings end with a closing round for final reflections.

A meeting process like the one described above can help you to get in the habit of relating to strategy in a new way. It also helps a team transition from static predict-and-control to dynamic steering, which takes more than just new principles or inspired leadership—it takes committed practice, within a system like Holacracy that embeds the shift into the core processes of an organization. With systems and processes upgraded in this way, most organizations can significantly deepen their capacity to navigate the complexities of the modern world, like a skilled cyclist steering down a busy street—gracefully, fluidly, consciously, and fearlessly.

Evolution Inside

In the opening chapter of this book, I made the claim that an organization running on Holacracy is not just evolved but *evolutionary*—able to adapt and learn and integrate by harnessing the tremendous sensing power of human consciousness. Holacracy, I proposed, achieves what Eric Beinhocker described as the key to doing better in business: "to 'bring evolution inside' and get the wheels of differentiation, selection, and amplification spinning *within* a company's four walls." Now that we've covered the mechanics of governance and the key principles of dynamic steering, I'd like to return to this essential point and explore how regular tension-driven governance can unleash evolution within a company.

"Evolution creates designs, or more appropriately, discovers designs, through a process of trial and error," writes Beinhocker. "Evolution is a method for searching enormous, almost infinitely large spaces of possible designs for the almost infinitesimally small fraction of designs that are 'fit' according to their particular purpose and environment." He describes evolution as a "search algorithm."[15] Modern evolutionary theory has identified four elements necessary for this search algorithm to work its magic and unlock the power of evolutionary design:

- an encoding of a design
- a way to express that code
- a way to vary the code
- a means of testing a design's "fitness" and amplifying fit designs

Let's briefly review how these elements show up in the biological realm we most commonly associate with evolution. First, there's an encoding. Our DNA encodes a design. Second, there needs to be a way to express that code. That's the role of our cells—they decode DNA and express the design it represents in the world. Third, there needs to be a way to vary the code. In mammals, that's sexual reproduction and random mutation. Fourth, there needs to be a means of testing a design's "fitness" and selecting fit designs to continue or amplify, while unfit designs are culled and left behind. In the biological realm this is known as natural selection—the process by which designs that are fit for their environment survive to reproduce and amplify, while their less-fit cousins diminish in number and eventually die off.

When these four elements appear and function together, a creative process is unleashed—the seemingly miraculous "design without a designer" that has given rise to all the diversity of life on this planet. Evolution takes a code, expresses it, tests the results to amplify fit designs and cull the rest, and varies the code to find even better designs. This process continues iteratively through ever greater refinement and creative emergence. The reason I call Holacracy "evolutionary" is that it brings this algorithm into an organization, through these same four elements.

When I say that Holacracy is evolution-powered, it's not just a metaphor. The governance outputs of an organization encode the organization's design—its roles, accountabilities, domains, and policies. In the operations of a Holacracy-powered company, we "role fillers" decipher that code and express it in the world. The results are tested against a fitness function, which in Holacracy is the organization's capacity to express its purpose with minimal waste. Fit designs are selected and kept, and to the extent a design is less than ideal for a given purpose, tensions will surface. It's our human capacity to sense and process these tensions through governance meetings that gives us a way to vary the code: we evolve the organization's design through Holacracy's governance process, one tension at a time. Each successive iteration through governance gives us a new variation on our organization's code, and each variation is further expressed and tested in an ongoing process, as evolutionary innovation carries our organization forward. With Holacracy, no single person designs the organization, and no single group sits down and designs the organization. Rather, an organization's design is an emergent result of an evolutionary algorithm—and that's a good thing, because when it comes to finding fit designs, evolution is much smarter than we are.

PART THREE

EVOLUTION
INSTALLED:
LIVING
HOLACRACY

ADOPTING HOLACRACY

> Large organizations of all types suffer from an assortment of congenital disabilities that no amount of incremental therapy can cure.
>
> —GARY HAMEL, "The Core Incompetencies of the Corporation"

I hope you've gotten at least a taste of what Holacracy is all about and how it can transform your everyday experience of the game of business. And, just maybe, you're intrigued enough to wonder: how can I shift my company to running this way? In this chapter, we'll cover some issues around the adoption of Holacracy, and I'll walk you through the process of launching Holacracy in your organization or team. I'll also share some ideas for what you can build on top of the foundation Holacracy provides; then, in the last chapter, we'll return to the topic of adoption and look at the challenges and shifts you can expect over your first year of practice.

One of the most common questions I hear from people learning about Holacracy is "Can I just adopt certain parts of the system, like the meeting formats?" It's an understandable question. Holacracy is a big shift, and I appreciate the desire to find a bite-sized way to start. But the simple answer is no.

Not if you want to get the benefit of a new paradigm. Not if you want to experience the deep transformation it offers. Sure, you could probably improve the efficiency of your meetings. But that, by itself, is not Holacracy.

Holacracy is a systemic change to a new power structure, and that's a binary shift: either power is held and delegated by a manager, or it's held by the Holacracy constitution. Either a manager declares what rules or processes will be used, or managers are bound by the constitution and no longer have the authority to make such declarations. Adopting pieces of Holacracy won't change the power structure, and the change in the power structure is where the real potential of Holacracy lies. To put it another way, if you try to adopt pieces of Holacracy, you still have to answer the question "Who chooses which pieces?," and that leads you right back to the existing power structure. That being said, if there's just no way you can adopt the whole thing right now in your current situation, don't worry—I'll share some advice for you in the next chapter, as many techniques and lessons from Holacracy can be quite useful even within a conventional organization. But the best place to start, if at all possible, is in making the shift to a constitutionally driven power structure.

That is going to be a scary leap, especially for any of your colleagues who haven't read this book. You will probably want to experience Holacracy in action before you try to convince others to invest your company's time and resources in such an endeavor. Fortunately, there are many ways you and your team can get a hands-on experience of the system before taking a decisive step. My company and others use a two-day executive workshop to help management teams explore Holacracy and the shift to a distributed authority system. Over those two days, we give an overview of Holacracy, run participants through governance and tactical meetings using their real, current issues and challenges, and explore what a rollout would look like in their organization and what initial circle structure they'd use. Aside from a custom experience like this, there are also many opportunities for people to get a taste of Holacracy or a deeper experience via public workshops and trainings. But whatever you do to explore the system and become confident that it's right for your organization, once you're ready to adopt, you need to take the whole package at once to get its true benefits.

Adopting the whole package doesn't mean you have to be able to practice it perfectly from the start. Compare it to learning to play a new sport—soccer, as we discussed before. When you're coaching six-year-olds to play soccer, you don't start them with just one or two of the rules and expect them to master those before they start playing the game. You have them follow all the rules as well as they can; they may not do it gracefully or with masterful skill, but they are playing soccer nevertheless. And that's how they will become skilled, with practice—by really playing the game, until perhaps one day they're playing at a high school level, or at college level, or in the World Cup. It's the same with Holacracy. You learn by taking on all the rules at once, at whatever level of skill you're at, and you improve by playing the game, with practice, as awkward as that might be at first.

Another option to consider is that while you can't really practice Holacracy by adopting only part of the rules, you *can* take on all of the rules in only part of the company, as when just one manager wants to adopt Holacracy without enlisting the broader organization. In that case, the manager adopts the Holacracy constitution and cedes power to it, but the "organization" the constitution refers to is just her team or department. An adoption like that in part of a company can be useful even if the entire organization eventually intends to follow suit. Especially in larger companies, it's not uncommon to see one department or division pilot Holacracy before the organization goes all in. Or the aim may be to build some internal skills and experience before a broader planned rollout. This is the approach Zappos took, piloting Holacracy in one department and then creating its own Holacracy Implementation circle to oversee the broader rollout and train facilitators.

Whatever the motivation for adopting in part of a company, be advised that doing so is likely to cause some friction. Once one team or department has these new pathways in place to process the tensions they sense, members may feel frustrated when they can't do the same outside the boundaries of their team. You'll also run into some challenges when Holacracy's new approach is partially incompatible with some of the organization's broader systems, such as conventional manager-driven compensation and firing processes. Several of the companies I've worked with that started with a pilot ended up accelerating company-wide adoption in order to resolve these and other challenges of "living in two worlds," as folks at one client organization began referring to it. Either way, you don't have to predict and control the adoption process entirely in advance; you can start from wherever you are, adopt the constitution, and adapt the roll-out process as you go, one tension at a time.

Holacracy for Communities?

Another question I often get asked is "Can I use Holacracy to run my social group, community, or movement?" Here the answer is nuanced. Holacracy is a governance system for an organization, not for a group of people—remember, the governance process is only allowed to govern the organization's work and its roles, not the people. In this usage, an "organization" is an entity that exists beyond the people, with its own purpose to enact and with work to do beyond just serving the people doing that work.

An organization

- has a *boundary* that defines its scope and property and processes, separate from the people involved—a "domain" that it controls and regulates
- has an *energetic exchange* with the outside world across that boundary; it provides something to/for the world, and receives something in exchange
- has a *purpose* it pursues, work to do for that purpose, and resources to deploy

If you have a legal entity that controls property (whether physical, monetary, or intellectual) and that performs some activity in the world, then you probably have an organization by this definition. If you're unsure—perhaps you're thinking of a social movement, a community group, or a club of some sort—then look at the criteria identified above and consider whether and how your potential organization meets them. What property is within its domain to control? What does it provide to the world, and what does it receive in exchange? What is its purpose and what work does it do to achieve it, beyond just serving those doing that work? Clear answers on these points will help you understand whether there's an organizational purpose, property, and work to structure and govern beyond the people. And if there is, exploring these questions will help you differentiate between the human community and the organizational entity, as Holacracy is solely for governing the latter.

Training and Guidance

While I've endeavored to cover as much detail as practical in these pages and to give real-life examples to illustrate the practices, I strongly recommend that any organization adopting

Holacracy seriously consider bringing in a qualified external coach to help with the transition. As you begin, the Holacracy coach needs to represent the constitution—he needs to know every rule and how to apply each in the moment, with skill, neutrality, and patience. And that's in addition to all the other business and coaching skills needed to shift an organization's power structure and help people learn new ways of influencing the organization and others.

That said, getting a qualified coach won't be practical for every organization, and I know that many people will want to adopt Holacracy without outside help despite this caution. If that describes you, consider getting as much hands-on experience and training as you can before you begin. There are plenty of public trainings on Holacracy available now, offered by several companies; find one that fits your budget and schedule and absorb everything you can before you dive in. Even if you have external support, or an internal expert, to guide you, the more that members of your team have a chance to experience Holacracy in a learning environment, the easier and faster the transition will be. In the words of Zappos' John Bunch, who led much of his company's Holacracy rollout, "Education is vital. At Zappos we developed a three-day training similar to HolacracyOne's Practitioner Training—400 people have been through it so far, and it has helped the rollout immensely."

If you'd like to get feedback about your understanding of how to operate in a Holacracy-powered company or facilitate a new circle, you can take a free online assessment at http://holacracy.org/assessment. It will test your knowledge of Holacracy's unique rules and power structure, as well as your understanding of the facilitation moves needed to enact them. In addition to an overall rating, the assessment gives question-by-question feedback, so you know where to focus for further study or other skill-building efforts.

Five Steps to Bootstrap Holacracy

Once you've got at least some training or a skilled coach available and you're ready to dive in, use the following process to bootstrap Holacracy in your organization and get started on the right track:

1. Adopt the Holacracy constitution.
2. Set up a shared system for governance records.
3. Define your initial structure.
4. Hold first governance meetings and run elections.
5. Schedule regular tactical and governance meetings.

1. Adopt the Holacracy Constitution

In order to adopt Holacracy as a new power structure for your organization (or team/department), you must first have whoever formally holds power clearly cede that power to Holacracy's "rules of the game." These rules are formally documented in the Holacracy constitution, and thus the first step to practicing Holacracy is to have the current power holder(s) ratify this document as the seat of power for the organization.

Who that ratifier is will depend on your existing power structure, and there may be many viable options depending on the extent you wish to deploy Holacracy. For an entire organization, it could be adopted via a formal board-level resolution or via a CEO policy without a board-level action. We usually recommend the latter, to avoid the extra complexity of getting board-level buy-in up front. If part of an organization is adopting Holacracy, the constitution could be ratified by an existing manager of the department, as long as he or she has the authority to define how work in the department will be structured and executed. The constitution could even be ratified by consensus or a democratic vote, if that's truly the current formal power structure in operation for your organization—although you're setting yourself up for trouble if you try to use this approach just to get buy-in, when it isn't the current formal power structure.

Whichever route is appropriate for your context, the key is to make the constitution's adoption formal and transparent. Put it in writing. For an adoption by a CEO or manager, download the PDF of the Holacracy constitution from holacracy.org/constitution and sign the one-page "Declaration of Adoption" at the end—then publish it. Everyone needs to know that the current power holder has formally ceded power. He or she can retain the right to "unadopt" Holacracy at any point and go back to the old way of running things, but not to override specific constitutional rules in the meantime. This is critical. For Holacracy to have the potential to work its magic, whoever adopts the system must agree to play by its rules and not be above the law, short of that pull-the-plug decision.

How you adopt the constitution—and at what level— determines the "anchor circle" for your Holacracy-powered organization. The anchor circle is the broadest circle in the new structure; it fully contains all work governed by the Holacracy constitution. Its purpose is defined as the purpose of the overall organization (or the part of it that's adopting Holacracy), and it has an automatic domain over all property of that organization and everything else the organization has the authority to control. If you are adopting the constitution via CEO policy, as I usually recommend at first, then your anchor circle is similar in membership and focus to your prior management or executive team, and is often called a General Company circle (or GCC).

The Holacracy constitution can also be formally adopted by a board of directors or equivalent and used to govern that board, in which case the board becomes the anchor circle and some special rules apply. (We'll cover Holacracy-powered boards later in this chapter.) The constitution can even be adopted in legal bylaws (or equivalent), further grounding Holacracy in the organization's fundamental power structure. I don't recommend this for an organization at the beginning of its journey with Holacracy; if it's ever something you'd like to consider, seek appropriate legal advice before messing with your bylaws.

However you go about adopting the constitution, you'll need to clarify the purpose of the organization and its anchor circle, and that job falls to the anchor circle lead link. More specifically, the anchor circle lead link is accountable for "discovering and clarifying the deepest creative potential the organization is best suited to sustainably express in the world, given all of the constraints operating upon it and everything available for its use, including its history, current capacities, available resources, partners, character, culture, business structure, brand, market awareness, and all other resources or factors that may be relevant." This is the constitution's formal definition of an organization's purpose. Before you proceed with your Holacracy kickoff, be sure the anchor circle lead link defines at least some initial purpose. And don't worry about getting the purpose "perfect" up front—it can always be improved or tweaked later, as tensions surface about the current definition and drive the need for more clarity.

2. Set Up a Shared System for Governance Records

To practice Holacracy, you'll need a place to store the organization's current acting governance (such as circles, roles, and accountabilities) and key operational information (such as metrics, checklists, and projects). These records are where people will find the expectations and authorities held by each role; if you are practicing Holacracy properly, every member of the company will refer to them often, even many times a day.

Using the right system to hold these records is critical. The entire power structure will be undermined if governance records are not clear and easy for everyone to access. Some companies try to repurpose a project management application to store the organization's governance structure. This *can* work, but most project management tools aren't designed for storing Holacracy-style governance records. Other companies customize a wiki or a similar intranet-like solution, which can be effective, especially if your customizations can enforce the right structure, fields, and editing permissions for governance data. You can also use GlassFrog, which as I mentioned earlier is a Web-based tool HolacracyOne created specifically for supporting Holacracy adoption, record keeping, and ongoing practice.

3. Define Your Initial Structure

Once you have ratified the Holacracy constitution and have a system set up for holding your governance records and key operational data, you are ready to determine your "initial structure," the set of role and circle definitions you'll start from. As you consider this, remember the *initial* structure is just that: a starting point. Holacracy is a living system for evolving your organizational structure over time, and the initial structure will change with every governance meeting. The organizational structure of one of our clients a year or so after Holacracy rollout usually looks nothing like the structure the client started with. This is true for most organizations using Holacracy, even small ones. So don't worry about perfecting the structure up front; just get something in place to start from so you can kick off effectively. The anchor circle's lead link has the authority to define the initial structure, and the lead link of every circle within may further tweak the initial structure in their circle before (and only before) its first governance meeting.

A typical approach to describing an initial structure is simply to define circles to represent whatever departments or teams you already have in operation, and then to define simple roles within each to capture the work that's already clearly happening. There's a trap to watch out for here: be careful to define the initial structure around what already exists and what already happens, not by what you think *should* exist or *should* happen. Don't get clever. Your goal is to ensure that everyone in the organization has at least one role to show up in, with at least a purpose or a single accountability attached to that role, and that those roles are grouped into half-decent initial circles. Stay grounded in what's already happening and, again, don't worry about perfecting it.

One final caution here for small organizations (with fewer than ten people or so): while you may have many roles, you probably have only one circle. If you think you have more, consider that each "circle" in your vision may actually be a role within a single General Company circle that just happens to work with other roles in that circle. In larger organizations, the same general caution is still useful: don't define a circle when you can get by with just a role that interacts with other roles (even those in other circles). It's a common pattern to see new organizations defining far too many circles, because novice Holacracy practitioners often think they need a circle anytime people need to work together. Remember, a circle is not for "working together," but for breaking down a single function (e.g., "marketing") into sub-functions ("blogging"; "advertising"; "events") that may be filled by different people.

Once you've determined your initial structure, the anchor circle's lead link should assign people to the various roles in the anchor circle, including assigning a lead link to each sub-circle, and then each of those lead links should do the same within their circles. Now you're ready to move to the next step: your first governance meetings and elections.

4. Hold First Governance Meetings and Run Elections

It's normally up to the elected secretary of a circle to schedule its governance meetings, but before a circle has run its elections, the task of scheduling an initial governance meeting falls to the lead link of each circle. The lead link may also act as default facilitator for that meeting, or may appoint someone else to do so. That person may be an external coach/facilitator or a trained facilitator within the company, even if she or he is not normally a member of the circle.

In this initial governance meeting, the lead link should add an agenda item to hold elections for at least a secretary and a rep link. The lead link may also call for a facilitator election at this initial meeting, although when a more experienced or trained facilitator is available to the circle, it's often advisable to hold off on electing an internal facilitator until the circle members are comfortable with the rules of the game and the facilitation process. In this meeting, use the integrative election process (see the constitution for details) to fill the elected roles, so that your circle is now ready to practice Holacracy.

5. Schedule Regular Tactical and Governance Meetings

The secretary of each circle should now schedule regular tactical and governance meetings for the circle. A typical frequency is weekly or biweekly for tactical meetings, and biweekly or monthly for governance meetings; at first, I usually recommend more frequent rather than less frequent meetings. While

this step may sound obvious, the would-be Holacracy imple-
menter would be well advised to pay attention to it. As simple as
it seems, in my experience a leading cause of failed Holacracy
implementations is simply not scheduling or holding the key
required meetings. Inertia can be a powerful force, and when a
team is still used to meeting and making decisions the old way,
it's very easy for members to let the new Holacracy practices
slip and just rely on old habits instead. Replacing those old
habits and building movement in a new direction starts with
doing the practice of regular Holacracy-style governance and
tactical meetings . . . and that starts with each secretary scheduling those meetings regularly and reliably.

If you follow the steps above, with some skilled facilitation
you'll be on the path to operating in Holacracy's new paradigm
and power structure. Don't worry if it feels awkward, slow, and
cumbersome at first—that's normal; in fact, if it's too comfortable, you're probably doing something wrong. It's a lot like
switching to a better operating system for your personal
computer—it may take a while to learn a new interface and
usability paradigm, but once you get the hang of it, you'll appreciate how much more quickly and smoothly you can get things
done. Similarly, when Holacracy is done well, meetings will
speed up dramatically and get very comfortable, but you'll
have to make it through a sometimes-painful learning process.
Like many new things, the practice of Holacracy will get a lot
easier with time and practice, if you have the patience and discipline to stick with it, and perhaps a little support along the way.

Beyond the OS: Installing and Creating "Apps"

I liken Holacracy to a new operating system because it changes
the fundamental power structure and governance paradigm for
your organization, without specifying how to structure all the

functions and processes your organization needs. Rather, the Holacracy constitution gives you an underlying platform, or a meta-process—a set of core rules for defining, evolving, and enacting your business processes over time. There are certain general business processes that most organizations need but that the constitution does not define, such as compensation and performance management systems, financial control/budgeting processes, and hiring and interviewing processes. To continue with our computing metaphor, these could be considered apps that run on top of an organization's underlying operating system, rather than features of the operating system itself.

Even the strategy meeting process described in Chapter 7 is not a part of the core Holacracy operating system; it's just an optional app. Any circle can "install" that app by adding an accountability on their secretary role for scheduling strategy meetings, and setting a policy that transfers the lead link's normal authority to define strategies into that meeting process. When I speak of apps in Holacracy, I mean a collection of related governance decisions like this, perhaps involving one or more roles, some new accountabilities, and a policy or two, that together enact some needed process or function.

Just as most computers need at least some basic apps in order to be remotely useful (email; calendar; Web browser . . .), most organizations also need at least some basic apps to function effectively. The business world is full of standard approaches—there's a rich suite of apps available for most common organizational functions, and plenty of business schools that regularly churn out graduates well versed in them. Of course, most of those apps were designed for companies running on the management hierarchy operating system, not on Holacracy. To go back to our metaphor, whenever you significantly upgrade your computer's operating system, you'll find that some of your apps may continue to work just fine, but others will need a replacement or an upgrade. You may also find that the new operating system offers new capacities, and you may want new applications to take advantage of them. Similarly, when you upgrade your organization to run on Holacracy, some of the ways you've done things in the past may fit just fine with the new system, but many others will become sources of tension, either clashing with some key shift in Holacracy or just failing to fully take advantage of its new capacities.

As an example, consider your organization's approach to defining compensation today. Once you've shifted to Holacracy, you'll probably find it feels somewhat nonsensical to approach compensation in a conventional manner—if there are no managers and no management hierarchy, and if roles are ever changing, how will someone's compensation be set? And if you think, "Well, the lead link can just do it," remember that people can fill roles in many circles with many different lead links. Even if you find a way around that issue, putting compensation decisions on lead links creates a pull back toward conventional power relationships. In short, if you continue with a compensation system that looks a lot like your current one, it's very likely you'll experience some significant tensions as a result, tensions that will impede your shift to Holacracy's new paradigm if you don't address them. In fact, any of your current processes that put key decisions on managers or otherwise rely on a management hierarchy may become significant sources of tension soon after you adopt Holacracy.

Fortunately, with Holacracy installed you've got a pretty good system for processing tensions and evolving your apps. So when you sense a need to improve a core system such as compensation, you can simply propose whatever governance is needed to come up with a new way of doing it, in whatever circle controls the relevant domain. You could design your own system, given your specific needs, but you may find it useful to check out what's already available in the broader community of Holacracy-powered organizations, and consider adopting a standard app built by someone else. To make this easier, HolacracyOne hosts a Holacracy "app store"—a website where Holacracy practitioners can share and find general apps designed for achieving certain goals or handling common functions. In fact, I suspect that much of the focus in the growing community of Holacracy practitioners over the next few years will be around developing novel apps to upgrade common business processes. I'm already seeing that happen in several of the client companies I'm working with, and we're always experimenting within HolacracyOne as well.

A good example of an app we've developed at Holacracy-One is the Badge-based Compensation App, which we use for determining who gets paid what, and why. In this app, each "badge" represents a specified skill, talent, or other capacity that's needed by the organization and its roles; a market value is tied to the badge. Partners in our company can earn these badges in recognition of their capacities, and compensation is tied to the most valuable badges a partner has earned and uses in her roles for the organization, using a standard formula. The badge definition and grant process are both tension driven, so anyone who feels a tension to get a new badge defined or to be recognized for earning one may kick off a process to assess adding or granting a badge. But no energy is wasted defining all the perfect badges up front or in assessing everyone's skills all the time. The badge system allows just-in-time clarity and continual evolution both in the key distinctions recognized by the compensation system, and in the individual placements and compensation levels within that system.

The app also distributes compensation decisions across multiple parties and processes, as different roles are involved with each step of badge definition, badge valuation, and tagging badges to roles. There can be a unique process for assessing eligibility for each individual badge, so different players will be involved in assessing the grant of each kind of badge. Some badges may be granted on the basis of certain facts or external authorities, as, for instance, when credentials are earned. Overall, this app changes the typical means of "progression" from a fairly linear climb up predefined tiers, to a process of building out a unique skill profile in any number of possible directions, including ones that don't need to be anticipated or planned for in advance.

This particular compensation app is a significant departure from conventional norms, and some organizations won't be ready for or comfortable with it. That's just fine; nothing about Holacracy requires you to use this system, or any other specific approach to compensation. Whenever tensions arise around your current compensation practices (and it's very likely they will), you can process them and find a step forward that's right for your organization. Perhaps you just create a role that sets salaries for everyone in the organization using their best judgment and whatever salary tiers already existed, but you keep that salary-setting role entirely separate from any lead link role. That would represent a step forward because it puts an explicit system in place using Holacracy. And it still helps to break the common initial conflation of "manager" and "lead link," while freeing people to fill roles in many circles without wondering who will set their salary.

Zappos did something similar after a year or so of Holacracy practice, creating a "Contribution Evaluator" role with the authority to set compensation for people and an accountability for gathering input from everyone someone works with when doing so. Even a more modest step like that takes you beyond the conventional approach and serves to reinforce rather than resist the other shifts Holacracy enables. In fact, we liked

Zappos' approach so much as an initial step that we based a generic app on it and published that in the app store.

Another example of a Holacracy-compatible app came from a client who found tensions surfacing around the organization's performance management system. The system was initially based in an older paradigm, with those formerly called managers still evaluating their team members against the various elements of the job description the employee had been hired under. But now expectations were much more dynamic, as each governance meeting had the potential to reshape roles and change what people were really accountable for. On top of that, it was no longer clear what a "manager" was and why those people were filling this function. These difficulties inspired the client to create a new performance management app.

They built an internal software tool that allows any team member to give feedback on another team member's execution of each of her specific accountabilities in each role she fills. The tool pulled role definitions in real time whenever feedback was initiated, so the feedback was always based on up-to-date accountabilities even as the governance changed. When the role responsible for updating someone's salary was ready to evaluate performance, he could use this tool to seek input from everyone who was actually working with that person, in addition to reviewing any historically captured feedback over the months before the review. The tool also allowed individuals to proactively seek feedback for themselves at any point, by requesting that their fellow team members provide an evaluation on one or more of their current roles. This information would also be stored and remained available for their next performance review.

This approach reportedly worked quite well for them—but, again, it's just one possibility. You'll need to find or develop the right apps for your organization. In general, the best apps for a

Holacracy-powered organization are those that take advantage of the operating system's unique capacities and work with them rather than resist them. In other words, they are compatible with Holacracy's flexible, dynamic organizational structure and its shift to distributed power and to having people fill many roles in several circles—they honor the differentiation of role and soul, and they don't rely on managers or old hierarchies. Some of your existing systems may be just fine and tension free, at least for a while, in which case you don't need to change them. If or when tensions do surface, just process them via Holacracy's governance system and change something—evolve your organization's apps over time, guided by real tensions.

A Holacracy-Powered Board

If your organization has chosen to adopt Holacracy through a CEO policy, then your board of directors or equivalent won't be notably affected, at least at first. But it's possible to use Holacracy at the board level as well, whenever that step makes sense to you, and the constitution includes some special rules to help you get the most out of board-level adoption. These rules also open up some interesting new possibilities for board-level representation and decision making, and may even shift how you think about the role of a board.

First, let's look at how a Holacracy-powered board is structured. Typically, when a board adopts Holacracy it becomes the organization's anchor circle, while delegating most of the day-to-day work to a General Company circle—often the board's sole sub-circle. The board appoints a lead link to the GCC, in the usual way, but the board itself operates without a lead link. The constitution allows a boardlike anchor circle to forgo a lead link. In addition to the usual processes Holacracy defines for a circle, the constitution provides a special rule in this case:

authorities and decisions that usually vest with a lead link are instead made via the Integrative Decision-Making Process, across all circle roles. This structure is probably close to what was in place before Holacracy—there are usually multiple directors on a board but no sole power holder with authorities similar to those of a lead link. What will likely be different is that the board will now have a much clearer and more effective process for how it functions, makes decisions, and delegates authority to its roles or to the GCC.

Before decisions can be made, however, a role for each board member must be defined. In the absence of a lead link, the constitution requires at least one cross link instead, and each formal board member will typically fill a cross-link role, possibly in addition to other board-level roles as well. If you recall, cross links are Holacracy's third type of link, typically used to invite an external entity to be represented within a circle. In this case, each of the board's cross links can represent the purpose and interests of another organization or a stakeholder group.

You could choose to have just a single cross-link role representing the organization's investors, with each board member assigned to it. In that case, the board structure would look much like a conventional board, just with better decision-making processes. However, you could also choose to have multiple cross-link roles, with some representing major contexts or stakeholder groups relevant to your organization other than investors, and that's where things get particularly interesting.

Traditionally, a board represents the economic interests of the shareholders (in a for-profit entity), or the organization's social purpose (in a nonprofit entity). In recent years, much has been written about the power of for-profit companies shifting to a "stakeholder orientation," where the organization focuses on serving all of its key stakeholder groups, not only investors:

key vendors; customers; employees; the local community; the environment. But, while many organizations have now adopted this ethos, their board structures have remained largely unchanged. And that actually makes sense, because a multi-stakeholder board in a conventional board power structure could easily devolve into a deadlock or a "tyranny of the majority." Even John Mackey, the CEO of Whole Foods, who's a champion and model practitioner of a stakeholder orientation, told me over lunch one day that he cautions against multi-stakeholder boards because they tend to diminish investor protections, when investors are already legally last in line behind other stakeholders for getting paid.

With Holacracy in place, however, a multi-stakeholder board might just become achievable and effective without significantly diminishing investor protections, thanks to the power of Holacracy's rules and its integrative governance process to ensure all tensions and objections get processed, even those coming from a minority voice. It's too early for me to make this assertion from experience—there just aren't enough cases yet—however I think it's an intriguing possibility.

An even more interesting possibility arises when there's another organization in your ecosystem that relates to your purpose or one of your stakeholder groups. You could invite that other organization to appoint a link to your board, creating a cross-organization cross link. For example, in addition to cross links representing investors, customers, and the organization's partners/employees, perhaps you'd invite another organization representing your industry or a relevant broader movement to appoint a cross link into your company—and maybe you'd ask for one back into theirs in return. If, in this way, your stakeholders had a more direct influence in your company, perhaps they could help the organization be a more constructive and trustworthy citizen in its world, and better express its own purpose in the process. Again, this is totally speculative. It could turn out to be a terrible idea, so proceed with caution if you choose to experiment with it. However we get there, though, I see a lot of potential in an ecosystem of purpose-driven organizations intertwined in healthy marriages with other purpose-driven organizations, all of them processing tensions across organizational boundaries.

However you choose to populate your board, Holacracy also reframes the purpose of the board's stewardship of the organization. With Holacracy adopted at a board level, the board does not exist to steward the company for the sake of its shareholders, or even for the sake of all of its stakeholders, but rather to steward it for the organization itself—in other words, for expressing the organization's purpose. Interestingly, this makes the distinction between for-profit and nonprofit less relevant. Organizations running with Holacracy are first and foremost purpose-driven, regardless of their tax structure, with all activities ultimately being for the sake of realizing the organization's broader purpose. Every member then becomes a sensor for that purpose, and the rules of Holacracy's governance process ensure that no individual interest can dominate.

With a diversity of perspectives in place and a process to integrate them, the board is now poised to tackle questions both difficult and deep. What does the world need this organization to be, and what does it need to be in the world? What is its unique purpose, its contribution to bringing something novel to life, to furthering creativity and evolution? The needs of shareholders and other stakeholders remain important constraints, but with Holacracy installed it is this deeper purpose that ultimately rules and pulls the organization forward. Like parents raising a child to find its own identity, the board guides the organization on its own path in life, toward finding and expressing its own deepest creative impulse, in harmony with all its relevant stakeholders.

When Holacracy Doesn't Stick

Holacracy isn't for everyone; I've certainly seen organizations where it just didn't stick, and there have been enough for me to notice certain patterns. Let's take a look at the three most common scenarios, which I've dubbed "The Reluctant-to-Let-Go Leader," "The Uncooperative Middle," and "The Stopping-Short Syndrome."

The Reluctant-to-Let-Go Leader

The critical step for a leader transitioning to Holacracy is to let go of power and allow the process to distribute the authority he or she once held throughout the organization. Because this power shift is essential, Holacracy's adoption will fail when the leader is just not ready to take the leap. It's understandable that many hesitate, especially those who have invested a great deal in shepherding their companies this far. Most, with the right support, do navigate this delicate transition, but for some it is just too much. Sometimes the leader of an organization is just not ready to go back to being a "beginner" who must learn a new way to hold authority and influence others.

Often, such a leader simply stops playing ball. He or she may give lip service to the principles of Holacracy, but continue to act in the old way and not really honor the new rules of the game. The resulting dissonance can't go unnoticed for long. In fact, what's interesting in these cases is that when a company has already started practicing Holacracy, the gap between the leader's words and actions is highly visible. Unlike in a traditional structure, where the rules of the game are usually implicit in the culture, and misalignment can be insidious, in Holacracy there is a natural transparency, with one explicit and cohesive set of rules laid out in the constitution. This makes it much more clear to everyone when someone is not following those rules.

At that point there are two choices. As I explained earlier, once a leader formally adopts the Holacracy constitution, he or she lets go of the right to change the rules, but does retain the ability to pull the plug and reject the whole thing. Some leaders do find the strength to let go at this point, but it's also the point at which the adoption can come to a pretty sudden stop.

I don't mean to be too critical of these leaders—handing over power to a new and unfamiliar process is a big step, and many have good reasons for deciding not to do it. One founder of a small start-up told me that he feared his organization and team just weren't mature and stable enough to self-organize effectively without strong leadership at the helm. Like a parent who fears his child is not strong enough or healthy enough to leave home just yet, this CEO wanted to wait until his company and its management team had gained more traction and experience before continuing with such a big change. I've seen Holacracy work beautifully in those kinds of environments, so I was a little skeptical, but I respected his decision: he knows his company and team better than I do, and it's his call to make. In fact, when the transition gets tough for my CEO clients, I'm often the one reminding them that they can drop Holacracy at any point; I'll even encourage them to at least consider that option. Better they stare the choice in the face and make it consciously, whatever side they land on, than that they subtly undermine the effort because they're not committed to the shift it requires.

The Uncooperative Middle

In another scenario I've seen a few times, the CEO is committed and is playing by the rules, but a layer of executives one level below is uncooperative, if not openly resistant to the shift. Some degree of reluctance and skepticism is normal and to be expected early in an adoption—in fact, it's often a healthy sign of care for the organization. But if Holacracy is to succeed, the organization will need to end resistance and ensure its members align with the new rules as much as they can, starting with those in former power positions who could otherwise undermine the shift.

Ending this resistance is more art than science. It usually takes a combination of clear messaging and leadership by example from the CEO; the right coaching and support to help former executives learn how to use the new rules to get work done; and updated human systems (apps) that reinforce the new rules and discourage working around them. Usually, if these are in place, resistance dies down. When, sometimes, it doesn't, the holdouts are usually executives who are really set in their old ways and doing quite well in that paradigm, though I've also seen diehard resistance from those early in their career who climbed the corporate ladder quickly. If just one or two people are balking, peer pressure can often sway them, or they may choose to move on, but if there is a large critical mass of uncooperative executives, the Holacracy adoption can grind to a halt.

One CEO, who faced a rebellion like this from the majority of his top executives and who eventually backed down, abandoning Holacracy altogether, admitted that "I was just spending too much political capital trying to get my executive team to stick with it." He decided to cut his losses and get back to running the company in a way his key executives would support.

I believe scenarios like this are particularly likely in organizations where there is less cohesion among the top team, or
perhaps just less cultural cohesion overall; such a context leaves
more room for resisters to work against the overall direction of
the company. Ironically, these are the companies that could
probably benefit most from a system like Holacracy, because
it would provide a cohesive process without requiring the
individuals to work out all their differences overnight.

In a more cohesive company, it can be easier to make the
shift, but even the most aligned and unified teams sometimes
find themselves fragmenting when they face the insecurity of
a paradigm shift like the adoption of Holacracy, and it's not
necessarily a sign of weakness that they're unable to make that
shift. Sometimes the moment just isn't right, or the system isn't
a fit for that particular team.

The Stopping-Short Syndrome

This is perhaps the most insidious scenario. It usually happens
in companies that think they have already succeeded at installing Holacracy. For a while, everything seems better—meetings
become more efficient, people better understand their roles, there
are avenues to process tensions, and a general entrepreneurial
spirit pervades the office. And then, slowly and almost imper-
ceptibly, the change starts to fade. People start (or continue)
looking to former managers to give direction and offer a nod of
approval before they make key decisions. Former managers
start (or continue) acting like managers, and slowly stop pay-
ing attention to the outputs of governance meetings. Everyone
starts (or continues) making one-on-one agreements, outside
of governance meetings, about how to work together, and uses
governance just to formalize those decisions . . . and then,
eventually, not at all. Yes, the meetings are still better, but is

the experience of working in the organization really that much different than before?

Companies like this end up, often without even quite realizing it, with only a fraction of the benefits Holacracy can offer. Some will continue to claim they're practicing Holacracy, but at best it's Holacracy Lite—a surface-level improvement in efficiency and clarity without the deeper paradigm shift.

Usually, this happens because the adoption process stalled somewhere along the way, before Holacracy was fully established as a replacement power structure. Most commonly, the decline starts after the basic pieces are in place—the constitution, the roles, the meeting processes—and it's time to start upgrading old systems and processes that are no longer highly compatible with the new power structure. This is where Holacracy's apps come into play—it's at this point that you need to rethink the way you do things like hiring and firing, or compensation. If you stop short of dealing with these difficult questions and finding appropriate solutions, you'll end up with Holacracy meeting processes overlaid on a power system that remains mostly unchanged. If "former" managers still have autocratic power to fire people and to set compensation, for example, it's difficult for team members to break old habits and take the risk of owning their authority and challenging managers in the ways that are essential to Holacracy's power shift.

To take Holacracy all the way, it's essential not to lose sight of the ultimate objective, which is a peer-to-peer distributed authority system. To get there requires commitment to making sure the change is reflected not just in the kinds of meetings you hold, but in the way power is held and used day to day, and in the core human systems and processes of the organization. Without that commitment, you'll end up with something that's just a little better than what you had before and that, in most cases, becomes unsustainable. It's just too easy to backslide, unless you commit to rooting out the old, lingering shadow power structure and reinforce the new power structure in tangible ways.

It's also essential to keep in mind that many organizations that fall into this pattern still feel good about the changes they've made and experience many positive results. But I hate to see people miss out on the full benefit of the investment they've made in adopting Holacracy.

I've seen the stopping-short scenario combine with the "uncooperative middle" to create a particularly disappointing failure. The CEO of the organization was fully on board and enthusiastic, but perhaps a little overconfident about what the change was going to require. His executive team was skeptical, a little reluctant, but willing to give Holacracy a try. At first, all seemed to be going well enough. People were getting it, meetings were going more smoothly, work was getting done more efficiently, and the naysayers seemed to quiet down a bit. But the shadow power structure remained strong, with former managers still acting largely like managers behind the scenes. On top of that, the team members who controlled key human systems weren't interested in changing them, which exacerbated the problem and allowed the shadow power structure to continue to control many functions. The CEO and perhaps one or two others might have been able to resolve these issues with time and energy, but the organization was dealing with so many other challenges at the time that this one didn't get much attention.

After many months of what looked like steady progress, the cracks were beginning to show. People were starting to wonder how much had really changed and to question whether they really needed all these rules. Ironically, the executives who had resisted upgrading key systems used this as leverage to push for rejecting Holacracy altogether, by pointing out all the challenges they faced because the half-done implementation was missing key pieces. Eventually the resistance was just too much, and even the committed CEO had to call it quits before distracting himself and his key team further.

These three scenarios, or some combination of them as in the story above, are the ones I most commonly see among Holacracy adoptions that fail. There's probably a fourth scenario, which I don't observe directly because it happens in companies that don't build enough internal capacity to facilitate a successful adoption in the first place. In these cases, people tend to underestimate the scale of the shift and approach it overconfidently and undersupported, or simply miss enacting key rules that hold the whole system together.

This being said, a majority of the Holacracy implementations I've witnessed seem to result in lasting transformation, at least when a clear commitment to change combines with solid external support or internal expertise. But it's useful to understand the patterns that result in failure, so we can avoid the more common pitfalls, navigate the challenges, and ultimately reap the benefits of a peer-to-peer distributed authority system that liberates our creativity, autonomy, and adaptability.

IF YOU'RE NOT READY
TO ADOPT: MOVING TOWARD
HOLACRACY

> The limits of my language mean the limits of my world.
>
> —LUDWIG WITTGENSTEIN, *Tractatus*
> *Logico-Philosophicus*

At the end of my presentation at a recent business conference, a man in his late twenties rushed over to speak with me as soon as I left the stage. I recognized his face, because he'd been sitting right in the front row, listening intently and taking notes as I talked.

His question was one I'd heard many times: "Is there a way I can use some parts of Holacracy without having to adopt the whole system?" I gave him my usual answer, the same one I've given in this book: "I'm sorry, but no. Holacracy is one whole interwoven system. If you try to take part of it without the others, you won't get the benefit of the paradigm shift. To experience the power of Holacracy, you need to take the whole package."

The young man looked disappointed. "There's no way I can do that," he replied. "I'm just a middle manager in a very traditional large company, and there's no way I can convince my bosses to completely reorganize and let go of their power, especially to a system they've never heard of. I doubt I'd even get approval to use Holacracy in just my department. But there has to be something I can do—some simple ways I can move my own working habits and the way I manage my small team a little bit closer to Holacracy."

His sincerity left me a bit unsettled. I stood by my original answer—Holacracy does work only when adopted as a complete system, even if only in a small part of an organization. But was that going to be the end of the conversation? Was Holacracy only going to be relevant for those with the power to call the shots at an organizational level? Did it have nothing to offer an inspired individual with limited power who wanted to do what he or she could to make a difference personally? That didn't feel good. I'd been that guy once, with layer upon layer of management above me, none of whom had time to listen to my concerns and ideas, let alone process my tensions into meaningful change. Back then, if I'd heard someone speak about a paradigm shift like Holacracy, and had wanted to start using it in whatever small ways I could, would I have accepted no for an answer?

I did ultimately offer my questioner some suggestions about what he could use from Holacracy to improve his current work. Then I reached out to my network to ask what others were using from Holacracy when they weren't able to apply the full system. I now believe there's quite a bit that's useful even without the full transformation; in fact, I realized I had been benefiting from aspects of Holacracy in my own personal relationships and in other environments that weren't practicing the whole system.

After these experiences, I resolved to build a more satisfying answer to this common question, and to share it in this book—and that's the point of this chapter. It comes, of course, with the same caveat I gave my friend from the conference: using pieces of Holacracy isn't using Holacracy, and if there is any possibility for you to adopt the whole system, I would almost always recommend doing so. However, if you're working in a company that simply can't, or won't, consider a wholesale adoption at this moment, here are some ways that the lessons of Holacracy may be able to benefit you and your team—and perhaps, down the road, inspire others in your company to consider becoming a Holacracy-powered organization.

My advice for those who aren't yet able or ready to fully adopt Holacracy falls into four categories:

1. Change your language, change your culture.
2. Rewrite your role descriptions.
3. Work *on* your organization, not just *in* it.
4. Streamline your meetings.

If you're able to take any or all of these steps, I suspect you'll notice a difference pretty quickly, at least on your own or within your small team. Be warned, however, that you will probably also become more acutely aware of how anti-Holacracy the corporate culture and structure around you is, in contrast with the new culture and habits you are beginning to cultivate. But perhaps others will notice the same thing, and you'll find allies in (eventually) bringing Holacracy to the company as a whole.

Change Your Language, Change Your Culture

They say actions speak louder than words, but sometimes we have a tendency to overlook the power of the words we choose. Language is commonly seen as the verbal expression of culture, but language can also create culture. In developing Holacracy, I've spent a good deal of time choosing terms that carry the meaning I want to convey, and that don't trigger old, habitual responses and associations. I've often heard from experienced Holacracy practitioners that they find these terms so helpful they've even started using them outside the workplace, changing the culture in their families or other relationships as well—in fact, I've done that myself. Try adopting some of these terms in your daily communications with your team and see how it changes your experience of working together.

Tensions and Tension Processing. Try replacing the language of "problems" and "solutions" with "tensions" and "processing." Human beings seem to be wired to put off dealing with things we perceive as problems to the last possible moment, so the use of this "negative" language around issues in business can create a culture of avoidance or unnecessary trepidation. "Tension," as used in Holacracy, is a neutral term that simply means *the feeling of a specific gap between current reality and a sensed potential.* A tension is not a "problem" and it doesn't necessarily need a "solution"; rather, it points to an opportunity to move the way things are in the present moment a little closer to the way things *could* be—which is usually a change for the better. Holacracy uses the term "processing" to describe this, avoiding the idea that there is a fixed and final result and instead conveying an open-ended journey of continual improvement and adaption.

Proposals Rather Than Problems. A shift that goes hand in hand with the one I've just described is to get into the habit of offering "proposals" rather than just lamentations. When you feel a tension, take the next step and ask yourself: "What would improve this situation? What could I propose?" Encourage your team to do the same. The proposal doesn't have to be a perfect "solution"—it's a way to start the conversation from a proactive, creative place, rather than a negative one.

Any Objections? Next time you find yourself seeking buy-in from your team around a decision, experiment with changing the way you communicate. Don't ask, "Does everyone agree?" or "Does everyone like my proposal?" Those questions set you up for a long and tedious discussion. Instead ask, "Does anyone see any objections to this proposal?" And define an objection as "a reason why this proposal would cause harm, or move us backward." Another way to phrase the question would be "Does anyone see any reason why this isn't safe enough to try, knowing we can revisit the decision if it doesn't work?" This simple shift in language can save a tremendous amount of time, and make your decision-making process much less cumbersome.

Roles versus People. When you're assigning actions or projects to a member of your team, try referring to those actions or projects as being assigned to the particular role that person is filling. This helps to decouple the often fused "role and soul" and thus to defuse the tensions that sometimes arise out of that conflation.

Dynamic Steering. You may also find the language of dynamic steering, which I explained in Chapter 7, helpful in shifting your team from a predict-and-control mind-set to one that is more responsive and adaptable, with less analysis-paralysis.

Rewrite Your Role Descriptions

Any organization, whether it's using Holacracy or not, needs to make it clear who owns what and who is accountable for what. You may be able to adopt Holacracy's style of defining roles (see p. 40 for details) even if you're not adopting the whole system. Remember, a role is not a person, and one person can—and probably does—fill several roles. Differentiating these roles and the accountabilities they carry can go a long way toward making expectations explicit and avoiding treading on other people's toes. If you're a manager, you can do this for your team, or you can simply do it for yourself, to clarify what is expected of you, and to explicitly describe the many hats you wear, probably one on top of another.

I recently heard a story from a colleague about a subsidiary of a large, traditional organization with a very conservative culture that decided to "only" clarify roles and accountabilities, and to occasionally discuss tensions so as to make implicit expectations visible and to amend those roles and accountabilities. Even using this one piece of Holacracy had gratifying results: the company saw a significant decrease in expenses incurred from bringing in external organizational-development consultants, and a dramatic reduction in the time people spent in meetings.

To begin clarifying your own or your team's roles, simply break down your own work or the work in your team into discrete chunks, and then describe each one with clear accountabilities, phrased as "-ing" verbs. For example, you may have always thought of your job as "Marketing Manager," but in fact you may fill several discrete roles within that broad domain. You're a Website Manager, Storyteller, Copywriter, Copyeditor, and whatever else, and each role has its own distinct set of related accountabilities.

One word of caution about role definitions: within the Holacracy system, roles are constantly evolving through the governance process so the descriptions stay relevant and useful. In the absence of that process, the danger is that your role definitions will quickly become obsolete, like the traditional job descriptions that sit in a drawer gathering dust, far removed from the needs and realities of people's day-to-day activities. Roles are only as useful as they are real, so make sure you keep revisiting and updating them—which leads to my next piece of advice.

Work *On* Your Organization, Not Just *In* It

Don't fall into the classic trap that Michael Gerber, author of *The E-Myth*, identified as catching most entrepreneurs: working *in* your business rather than *on* it. You may not be an entrepreneur with the power to call the shots in your own company, but wherever you sit in the organizational hierarchy, there are ways you can work on the business as well as in it. Or to put it in the language of Holacracy, you can engage in governance.

If governance is not something you're accustomed to doing, it's important to carve out time and space for the process that is separate from your operational work. One simple way you might use this time, as mentioned just above, is in reviewing and updating your own role descriptions. You can also spend time identifying tensions you've experienced and coming up with simple proposals to process them that you might suggest to your team or manager. If you're a manager yourself, you might also review and update your team's role descriptions on the basis of the actual experience of working together. You may not be able to call a governance meeting, but if you dedicate time and attention to improving the way your team works together, you're engaging in governance.

You can also make it known that you'll be doing this, and invite your team to let you know whether they feel tensions that could inform your process. This will help everyone start developing an awareness of governance issues, and foster a more entrepreneurial mind-set around their own roles and responsibilities. Try the approach Gonzales-Black of Zappos took: encourage your colleagues to ask themselves, "What would I do if this were my business?"

Streamline Your Meetings

If there's one thing most people from top to bottom in an organization tend to share, it's a hatred of wasting hours in long, inefficient meetings. And if there's one thing almost everyone who practices Holacracy remarks on eventually, it's how much relief they feel thanks to the streamlined, efficient meeting formats. While some of Holacracy's meeting processes, such as the governance meetings, don't work well outside of a company that has adopted the constitution, others may be useful anywhere, in whole or in part.

The best example is the tactical meeting format (see p. 95). Holacracy's approach to "triaging" issues, focusing on "one tension at a time," helps meeting participants quickly get to a workable solution that satisfies the person who raised the tension in the first place. I've heard of companies that successfully used this format in place of their general staff meetings even though they were not running on Holacracy. If the full meeting process is too much, here are some elements you can add to any meeting you're in.

Check-in and Closing Rounds. These can be easily added to the beginning and end of almost any meeting. Their purpose is simple: the check-in round allows all present to notice and share whatever is on their minds that might be distracting them, so that the team is more present and focused, ready to move on to business at hand, while the closing round gives each person an opportunity to share reflections about the meeting. Just remember, in both rounds, people speak one at a time, with no discussion or response allowed. This is essential, to avoid your meetings devolving into personal discussions and to create a "safe space" for people to open up.

On-the-Fly Agenda Building. Rather than going through a preset list of items that you think you should talk about, try driving your meetings with agendas built on the fly, in the meeting. This limits the agenda to items that someone feels enough tension about to bring up right then and there, and thus ensures that anything you spend time on is actually worth it, at least to someone.

The "What Do You Need?" Approach. When dealing with an agenda item raised by a team member, it's always helpful to start with the question "What do *you* need?" This keeps the discussion focused on resolving the issue at hand. It also helps to remind everyone that the only goal is to satisfy the person who raised the issue, without being diverted into other people's related concerns. You'll know you're ready to move on when the person who added the agenda item can answer yes to the question "Do you have what you need?," even if other people aren't satisfied. Their concerns can be dealt with as separate agenda items if necessary—which leads to the next element you may find useful.

One Tension at a Time. This simple rule works wonders for streamlining a meeting and keeping it on track. It's all too easy to start off addressing one issue, then find yourselves diverted by a half dozen related concerns, as everyone piles pet peeves on top of the original tension. The result is usually unsatisfactory for everyone, as often not much gets effectively resolved. Sticking to one tension at a time, and insisting that related concerns become separate agenda items, ensures that each one gets the attention it needs.

Integrative Decision Making. I offer this final suggestion with caution. The IDM process used in Holacracy governance meetings (see p. 72) can, in some circumstances, be used as a means of general collaborative decision making—but carefully. In Holacracy, this process is only used in governance, for making specific types of decisions, and the Holacracy framework provides clear guidance for how those decisions can be changed, if need be, and what kinds of decisions the process is appropriate for. Without that scaffolding in place, the IDM process has limited usefulness. That said, it can be an effective operational decision-making process as well when you have big strategic decisions to make, or even smaller but still significant decisions into which you know you need to integrate multiple perspectives. A colleague told me that she adapted the IDM process to help a group of managers make a key operational decision, and in ninety minutes they managed to resolve an issue they'd been debating for the past five months. Just remember, don't try to use it for just any old decision—stick to the major ones that don't need to change often.

However you proceed with these ideas, remember to steer as you go. Even in a wholesale adoption, the goal isn't to change everything right away. Let the tensions guide you. When you become aware of ways in which your current systems are holding you back, ask yourself, "What would work better? Is there a way I can apply what I've learned from Holacracy to improving this situation?" When you start to see a next step emerging—one that is achievable and will help move the work forward—take it, and see what happens next. Wherever you start, I hope that you will one day have the opportunity to experience the paradigm shift of working in—and on—an organization powered from top to bottom by Holacracy.

10

THE EXPERIENCE OF HOLACRACY

> We can never really be prepared for that which
> is wholly new. We have to adjust ourselves, and
> every radical adjustment is a crisis in self-esteem.
>
> —ERIC HOFFER, *The Ordeal of Change*

"I barely recognize my own company now," one executive told me. "Since adopting Holacracy, it's almost like we've been acquired by a different company."

I've heard many variations on that sentiment from leaders who have adopted Holacracy in their organizations. Usually it's said with a mixture of exhilaration and disorientation in the early stages of adoption; eventually the disorientation gives way to a sense of liberation that is palpable. It's hard to convey in a few short pages the substantial change that these leaders are experiencing—as is anyone else who shows up in a newly Holacracy-powered workplace. Imagine if you got into your car in the morning, and suddenly there was no steering wheel in front of you, no gear lever next to you, and no brake or accelerator pedal beneath your feet. Instead, you face an unfamiliar set of dials, buttons, and sticks that you have no idea how to operate—and yet you've still got to get somewhere, and fast. Stranger still, the passenger seats have the same set of controls in front of them. This could be quite disorienting and maybe even disempowering: your long-practiced driving skills are suddenly no use to you. Yet, as you tentatively pull out of the driveway, you get a sense that despite its strange new control system, the car might now have capacities the old version never had. It takes you a while to get used to it, but slowly it becomes a joy to ride in, getting you where you need to go much faster and with less effort. I think that's often what it feels like to go from a traditionally run organization to a Holacracy-powered one.

In the course of helping numerous organizations adopt and install Holacracy, from small start-ups to reasonably large companies, I've watched and supported many people through the adjustment to a new control system and the paradigm shift it requires in how leaders approach their function in the organization. Each case is different, but I've started to notice some familiar themes. So while there really is no substitute for experiencing the shift directly, in this final chapter I will try to convey some of the essential ways in which your day-to-day experience might change if your organization started running with Holacracy, and some of the issues you might have to navigate as you transition into its system of distributed authority and dynamic governance.

Toppling the Hero

One of the most dramatic shifts plays out with the key leaders/power holders of the organization (founders, CEO, executives), as the relationship between them and the rest of the team is reconfigured and authority is redistributed throughout the organization. For these leaders, the shift I've been describing can present an existential challenge—but on the other side of that, there's an opportunity for tremendous relief and release.

If you're a leader who has been accustomed to holding a heroic role, using every ounce of your personal will and capacities to drive or carry the organization forward, you will need a new kind of heroism to let the old kind go. You may feel as if you're downshifting the efficiency and performance of the roles you used to fill. Now you have distributed the authority to people who may not have the capacities you have. Initially, you're likely to feel a dip in efficiency, productivity, and momentum. And you're accustomed to being responsible. Suddenly, you are not the only one driving the organization forward, and the limits of your team are more likely to affect your progress.

Of course, from another perspective, the organization is less constrained, because it is no longer completely dependent on you as a heroic leader and subject to the limits of how great a burden any one person can carry. Often, the intuition that they are approaching the limits of their individual capacities is what inspires leaders to seek a new organizational practice in the first place, to allow their companies to better scale beyond themselves. But as much as heroic leaders may sense this need, they are also usually embedded in the existing power structure and not fully aware of how much they are limiting the organization's ability to pursue its purpose—even as they are also one of the greatest champions of that purpose. As one of our clients shared, "The more I found out about Holacracy, the more I realized that it was the solution both to the problems I was facing at the time and to the problems I hadn't yet considered but would have inevitably faced had we stayed on the road we were on." When the heroic leader gets the first glimpses of what he or she was looking for, the reaction is often a combination of fear and relief.

This is the pivotal moment on the path to Holacracy adoption; if the leader is unable to see his or her own reactions with some degree of objectivity, and trust the process enough to let go, it can be a point of failure. Most leaders I've worked with, however, are able to move through this transition and discover the rewards that lie beyond the scary prospect of letting go. One leader described to me how she would catch herself reverting to what she called "power founder mode" when she felt insecure about things not being done the way she wanted them; but through her commitment to Holacracy, she was able to start resisting the temptation to wield autocratic power in this way and respect the sovereignty of other role holders. Slowly, she started to see that they were actually able to manage situations without her exerting authority, and she was able to relax and trust her team more. At the beginning, though, it's never easy to break the fusion between a leader and an organization.

I find this even more understandable when the leader is also the founder—the visionary who brought the organization into existence. But being the founder is not a prerequisite to overprotective organizational parenting. I worked with one CEO who had no particular attachment to the mission—he was a hired gun, brought in to get things on track—but who was nevertheless quite attached to the role of heroic leader. That was the way he had learned to add value in all of his previous organizations—through being a good, kind, warmhearted, personal father figure. A challenge to that identity was deeply disconcerting to him. It was touch-and-go for a while, but he hung in there long enough to see positive results, as a new spirit of autonomy and creativity emerged among his team, and they stopped looking to him as the father-boss to make everything better for them. This change became his inspiration to continue with the process, and ultimately he found it a relief to let go.

I confronted this same challenge in my own journey, as founder of the software company that incubated the early glimmers of Holacracy. Slowly, as I practiced the processes I had put in place, I got what I asked for, and it revealed to me that

I was deeply attached to being the heroic leader—the one who would take care of everything, the one on whom it all depended. I'm sure many parents have found a sense of meaning in raising their children that's similar to my experience in raising my company, and I'm sure some have faced a similar crisis of identity when those children grew up and no longer needed parental heroism. It was tough to see this pattern showing up in myself, and even tougher to let it go. My sense of identity had become partially fused with a story of myself as a conscious, empowering servant-leader, stewarding my company and my employees to greatness. It's a powerful image that our culture has elevated to heroic status—understandably, as it often reflects the best we can do in our conventionally structured organizations with their heavy reliance on centralized leadership. But for all the positive qualities of the heroic role, striving to fulfill it had become something of an ego trap for me as well—it had become a significant source of my self-esteem and a central pillar around which I was constructing my sense of identity and self-worth. Initially, that left me blind to its limitations and to seeing other possibilities that didn't rely so much on my own heroic, conscious leadership.

A limit I now see in this heroic-leader paradigm is that no matter how caring, charismatic, and selfless the leader may be, the whole system is limited by that leader's capacities. There is an expectation that such leaders will be superhuman—and, always, there is disappointment when they turn out to be less than this. When I found the courage to step beyond that role and to release control into a process that could manage the organization better than I ever could have, I experienced a surge of relief—I no longer had to try to be superhuman or pretend to be, either to myself or to others.

I also found that my own capacities were suddenly liberated in a way that surprised me. I had not realized how much energy

I was expending just trying to use my power appropriately, trying to be at my best and temper my reactions so I didn't disempower or suppress others. I was aware that other people were fundamentally vulnerable to my use of power, and this required a certain conscious attention and diligence on my part, to be an empowering and compassionate leader who left space for others. But to get there I had to be dialed down, not fully letting my sometimes-incisive perspectives and other capacities shine and have their impact. At other times I would drop the diligence—or just fail at it—and instead privilege driving a project forward with my own perspectives and insights. But this often came at the expense of empowerment and leaving space for others. It was a terrible dilemma, and I was stuck with an either-or choice when I wanted a both-and—I wanted to be able to drive forward with my own insights and strong perspectives without holding back, and at the same time create an environment where others had space and power without me getting in their way.

With Holacracy in place, I don't need to choose any longer. I can use my full capacity to drive forward without sacrificing empowerment, because no one is vulnerable any longer to my use or abuse of ultimate organizational power. No one has to listen to me unless governance says so, and they all have channels to process any tensions they feel as a result of my actions. It's a huge relief to be able to fully express my opinions and perspectives and to use them to drive my projects forward. Now I can make a strong case for something, I can fill roles I'm ready to lead and run with them, I can unleash my full capacity without worrying about steamrolling others in the process. And I no longer waste my energy trying to "empower others" in a fundamentally disempowering system.

Free from the constant pressure to be perfect, I can be myself, and those around me can do the same. The system even holds a space for me to be imperfect—to be having a bad day, to be stuck, to be overly attached to my own ideas—without destroying the power and capacity of others.

That being said, Holacracy certainly doesn't remove the value of me, or anyone else, being a conscious, aware, good leader. It just distributes that need across more people, and makes it a useful capacity, rather than an unattainable ideal. Holacracy doesn't rely on any one person's ability to be a consistently great leader; it relies on everyone's ability to be a good leader *sometimes*—and that also makes it okay that no one person will be a great leader all the time.

In this, we take on a peer-to-peer relationship rather than a codependent parent-child dynamic. We show up as partners, each responsible for the purpose of the organization and for our roles in actualizing that purpose. In HolacracyOne, this partnership is not just a change in the way we relate to each other, it's a legal reality. We've structured the organization so that we have no employees. Rather, everyone is a partner in a legal partnership governed by the Holacracy constitution, with a voice in the organization's legal power structure through Holacracy's governance meetings. Of course, it's not necessary for every company to make Holacracy legally binding like this; even when Holacracy is simply adopted as a policy, the impact is profound.

Holacracy's dramatic cultural shift comes at a price. For those who find it comfortable to give over their power to a leader who directs them and blesses their decisions, Holacracy means giving up that hiding place and being willing to take on authority and all the responsibility that comes with it—in a sense, to be more naked and exposed, more vulnerable, and to really *lead*, even if just in their role as one small part of the overall company. And for those who are attached, as I was, to being a good empowering or caretaking leader, Holacracy means letting go of that self-image and all the self-esteem it gives us—not to mention letting go of the desire to control everything. On the other side, you'll find a tremendous sense of creative freedom and a newfound ability to get your own work done, rather than constantly trying to parent everyone else.

The Holacracy coach Anna McGrath told me a story she heard from Rick Kahler, the founder of Kahler Financial Group, who had been working with Holacracy for about a year. "I arrived disheveled, tired, and almost late to a governance meeting yesterday from a trip to the East Coast," he told her. "There were six at the table, and I was the seventh person, almost the odd man out. I had no issues of any importance to share. As I watched the meeting unfold, it was clear my presence wasn't important to the process. Agenda items popped up from almost everyone and the magic unfolded. It was as if I was there as an observer. Don't mistake that as me not being part of the process, but *I was not the process.* The responsibility to 'carry' the meeting was totally nonexistent for me. Later, I got some feedback from another colleague who said, 'Don't take this the wrong way, but for the first time I didn't experience you as "big" in the meeting. You were just one of us. I looked around the table and I really felt like we were a team.'" For Rick, and many leaders like him, an experience like this is a great relief.

You might even find, as one client of ours recently did, that you can take a much-needed break. "Holacracy has enabled me to take the first real, off-the-grid vacation in, well, forever," confessed Phil Caravaggio, the founder of the industry-leading nutrition coaching company Precision Nutrition. "Essentially, because Holacracy forces you to clearly and explicitly define your roles and your work, it becomes ridiculously easy to then swap other people into those roles temporarily while you're away. The people filling the roles won't be able to do the same job I would do, but they do get clear direction on exactly what needs to be paid attention to. And there is no authority vacuum or confusion as to who's accountable for what. That's a completely unexpected and extremely welcome side effect of adopting Holacracy, because one of the main reasons I made the switch to begin with was the 'founder burnout' feeling my cofounder and I had started to experience."

Ultimately, Holacracy is empowering to everyone in the system, including the leader. But first—to go back to our metaphor of the car with new controls—you have to take a deep breath, figure out those unfamiliar controls, and back the car out of the driveway—while everyone else around you is doing the same.

Interestingly, one trend I've noticed with our clients is that leaders who are willing to let go sometimes expect me (or one of my colleagues) to pick up the heroic leader role as I help to facilitate the transition. When we start to work with the meeting processes, they expect me to read their emotions and those of their team, and adjust the process to suit their needs. When I hold firmly to the process, they feel affronted, as if I were expressing a personal lack of care for them and their organizational family. It takes a while for them to adjust to the fact that as a facilitator I am caring for the *process*, not for the individuals. I'm not letting myself be seduced into filling the power vacuum, but am simply holding the space for the process to do its work, by following the rules of the constitution. In the early stages, it's a messy process and no one is familiar with those rules. But it's not my job to mitigate that by becoming a surrogate boss, no matter how uncomfortable it may be.

The result is often that at first the process feels like leaderless chaos. In the initial governance meetings with one recent client, I was writing down verbatim the proposals people were bringing, even though they weren't expressed clearly and in proper governance form. And, predictably, they didn't make much sense. Later, when I raised the objection "Not valid," people started to get frustrated with me. "Why didn't you help me fix it or improve it in the first place?" But I simply wrote it down, and applied the process. Slowly but surely, the process itself will bring clarity and sense to what has been submitted. Eventually, people begin to put their trust in the process and in their own ability to use it, rather than in me, or their CEO, or anyone else.

The beauty of this redistribution of authority is that it removes the need for personal heroics to come from a manager, a consultant, or anyone. Once Holacracy is installed, the power on each team stops residing with a single heroic manager-leader and instead resides in the process, which is embodied in the constitution. But this does not result, as some may fear, in an aimless, inefficient, chaotic organization. In a sense, everyone becomes a leader of his or her roles. A participant in a training once captured this perfectly when he commented that, rather than moving from a leader-driven autocracy to a leader-less collective, which many companies have tried to do with limited success, what Holacracy does is to create a *leader-full* organization. Leadership becomes attainable, even a matter of course—it is what everyone does.

Uprooting the Victim

Leaders are not the only ones who can find the transition to Holacracy uncomfortable. In the parent-child dynamic that exists in most organizations, those who take on the archetypal role of child are often deeply attached to that mode of being, even if they are also frustrated by its disempowering dynamic. However much we all may complain at times about bad managers, I think most of us like being able to turn to a heroic leader to solve problems we don't know how to deal with ourselves, or just don't want to own and face. Holacracy breaks this dynamic for everyone, with interesting consequences.

As they are given authority over their roles, those who are used to being a long way down the organizational food chain often feel a discomforting sense of having nowhere to hide out anymore, and no one else to blame. Taking the position of the child or the victim, however disempowering it may be, also lets us off the hook. We can complain and grumble around the water cooler, but never have to really do anything about the tensions we feel. How could we? We don't have the power. But in Holacracy, that position is turned on its head. We *do* have the power—no matter where in the organization we sit, we have the power to process any tensions we feel into meaningful change. As Alexis Gonzales-Black at Zappos puts it, "Holacracy is not going to get rid of your problems; Holacracy is a tool that allows you to solve your own problems."[16]

Using that power can be scary at first, and it may take a while for people to trust that they won't be scolded or punished for doing so. However, Holacracy won't allow much choice—it's difficult to hide from empowerment when the organizational process around you continually shines a light on your hiding place. Holacracy makes it obvious that you can process tensions and are simply choosing not to; that you do have a voice and are simply choosing not to use it; and that there is no "them" holding all the power—just *you*. And it makes clear that not only do you have the power, but also, if you agree to fill a role and act as its steward, you also have the responsibility. The organization is depending on you, as its sensor, to give voice to the tensions you sense so that it can evolve.

Of course, we all still complain from time to time about things we don't like. But with Holacracy at play, we have much more of a choice. We can choose to waste our energy grumbling about the way things are, or we can get on with doing something about it. It can be quite a self-revealing process. When you no longer have the option to play the victim and

blame "them" or "the circumstances," you see your own resistance to reality simply for what it is. A meditation instructor
who went through a Holacracy training once commented that
the process was remarkably similar to what she teaches people
in meditation—how to notice their resistance to reality and
their attachments to perspectives. And like the practice of meditation, the practice of Holacracy isn't easy. It can be uncomfortable to have that inner mirror held up to all of your
resistances and not be able to unconsciously project them onto
others. But it is also more genuinely empowering than any other
approach I've come across. Holacracy calls on each individual
to inwardly step up and own his or her authority—a step that
is likely to be at times challenging, terrifying, and, possibly,
exhilarating.

Stepping into unfamiliar authority can be an awkward experience at first. With Holacracy, you don't need to seek consensus or approval for decisions that fall within the power of your
role to make. But some people find it hard to break this habit,
worried that they will offend or upset their colleagues by making decisions without asking everyone's opinion. An example
of this showed up recently in one company I was working with,
where Holacracy was just being introduced. The secretary of a
circle had scheduled biweekly governance meetings, but one
morning, the CEO announced that he would be traveling inter-
nationally and wouldn't be there for the next meeting, so it had
to be rescheduled. He was concerned that the meeting might
cover key topics that he should be involved in—an understandable concern for the leader of a company that was undergoing
such significant changes.

However, as I explained to the CEO, the Holacracy constitution gives the elected secretary the authority to schedule or
cancel a circle's governance and tactical meetings. Anyone can
give input about when to schedule, but the secretary has the

authority to take it or leave it, and is not required to seek it out. In this case, the secretary made a judgment call and decided to go ahead with the meeting. But interestingly, when the meeting began, she brought up the very first agenda item, which was a policy proposed to formalize her decision: "We meet every other Monday regardless of who can or can't make it."

What was fascinating about this moment is that the secretary already had all the authority to make that decision. She did not need a policy—in fact, all her proposed policy would do is *constrain* her authority to use her best judgment if she wanted to change her decision later. When I saw this, I realized she was feeling uncomfortable with embracing her autonomy and authority, and she was afraid of violating the comfort zone of others, particularly the CEO. This is common in the early stages of adoption. Most people are not used to having authority and don't understand that they can relax into it, knowing that the governance process gives everyone a chance to process any tensions that may arise as a result. The secretary wanted to preempt any tension that the CEO or anyone else might be feeling by making sure there was a consensus, which would help her feel more comfortable. The beauty of Holacracy, however, is that this kind of preemptive action isn't necessary. As I explained to her in our next coaching session, all she needed to do was to embrace her authority. If the CEO or anyone else felt tension about how she was using it, he could bring a proposal to the next governance meeting to set a constraint on how the secretary schedules meetings.

If people are feeling discomfort about not seeking consensus, or are apologizing for making certain decisions or for rocking the organizational boat, that's a good sign—a sign that they're starting to move into a new relationship to each other and to their own roles. Slowly, as people get more comfortable holding and using authority, they will stop feeling the need to apologize. Does the heart check with all the other organs before pumping blood around the body? Does the liver apologize to the stomach for filtering out harmful substances?

When this shift begins to more deeply take root, and you feel liberated from the dynamics of a parent-child relationship with a leader, a new kind of motivation can often get released. One person I worked with described it as "a powerful drive to operate at the very edge of my capacities—to stretch beyond and develop in new ways. That drive is no longer coming from having a boss breathing down my neck, but it's arising from my own sense that my roles depend on me, and the broader system depends on my roles functioning." This can become quite a potent cultural dynamic, as we inspire each other to step up and be the best we can be. I sometimes compare it with what I've heard from those who serve in the military—that sense of deep camaraderie that arises when you know you all depend on one another and each person embraces that absolute responsibility.

Moving Beyond a Personal Paradigm

As you approach a clear and transparent structure of roles and accountabilities, you may also become aware of a deeper paradigm shift. It will start to become apparent the extent to which decisions and expectations up till now have rested on the politics of personal relationships or on agreements between specific people. As the CEO of a client company put it, "Holacracy helped us transition from a culture where everything relied on specific people to one where things rely on roles and practices."

For most people, leaving behind the many negative manifestations of personal politics is ultimately a relief. But in many organizations there's a very positive side to the personal climate as well, and that's much harder to let go of—the relationships developed and grown within a supportive environment, and a human culture of care and connection. Those who have enjoyed this kind of environment are often understandably apprehensive when they first experience Holacracy. They've learned to navigate and use personal relationships to achieve an organizational result, and Holacracy requires they let go of the very thing that has made them effective. They'll also need a new mental model of what organizational life is all about and how individuals should show up in it.

To make this point, I often say flat-out: *Holacracy is not about the people.* This is one of the aspects of the practice that people have the hardest time swallowing, but it's fundamental. Holacracy doesn't try to improve people, or make them more compassionate, or more conscious. And it doesn't ask them to create any specific culture or relate to each other in any particular way. Yet precisely by not trying to change people or culture, it provides the conditions for personal and cultural development to arise more naturally—or not, when it's not meant to be.

I consider this one of the most beautiful paradoxes of Holacracy. And it is not an easy one to explain, especially nowadays, with the push for improving organizational cultures, developing individuals, and promoting more conscious leadership. Holacracy does its work on an entirely different level; it doesn't directly conflict with most of these efforts, it just puts in place a different underlying system, in which such initiatives are simply less of a key leverage point for needed change and where you get some of the same results without seeking them directly.

Holacracy is focused on the organization and *its* purpose—not on the people and their desires and needs, however positive these may be. Even in Holacracy's highly integrative governance meetings, which allow every individual to have a voice, the point is not to seek the personal consent of the people involved or ensure that they're personally happy with the decisions. Many of the rules of the governance meeting process are there specifically to ensure that the focus is only on what's needed for the organization to express its purpose, given the concrete needs of its roles, not on personal opinions, desires, values, goals, or anything else. Seeking people's consent or reaching consensus is not the required threshold for decisions to be made in a Holacracy governance meeting, and its nuanced rules will actually prevent that focus from intruding at all, or will quickly discard it if it does. Holacracy's systems and processes are about continually helping the organization find its own unique identity and structure to do its work in the world, while protecting it from human agendas, egos, and politics. Holacracy allows the organization to be more driven by its own unique purpose in life, like a child developing its own identity and goals beyond those of its parents.

When the David Allen Company was going through this transition, many of the people within were struggling with the shift to a more impersonal approach. They'd worked hard for years to build a very close, warm, intimate culture, and you could feel it the minute you walked into their building. It seemed like a really great place to work, where people trusted each other, listened to each other, and shared a deep connection. In the process of installing Holacracy, we were deliberately tearing out that carefully woven fabric of relationships from the way people did their work, and many people found the change quite jarring. But Holacracy wasn't removing all of their hard-won connectedness and trust, just moving it into a different space and liberating it from organizational matters.

At some point it really clicked for David, who put it into his own words: "What you're saying is that it is an inappropriate use of love and care to *use* love and care to get something done."

That has since become one of my favorite ways to describe this aspect of Holacracy. We're not dismissing or limiting a culture of love and care by installing Holacracy—in fact, we are making the domain of human connection *more* sacred, because we are installing a system in which we no longer need to lean on our connections and relationships to be able to process organizational tensions. Holacracy also has the reverse effect as well: it reduces the impact of organizational tensions on human relationships.

Some months later, reflecting on the transition his company had gone through, David made an interesting observation: "As we've distributed accountability down and through the organization, I've had much less of my attention on the culture. In an operating system that's dysfunctional, you need to focus on things like values in order to make that somewhat tolerable, but if we're all willing to pay attention to the higher purpose, and do what we do and do it well, the culture just emerges. You don't have to force it." What he and his team were discovering is that, far from suppressing the personal and interpersonal dimensions, Holacracy actually releases people to be more fully themselves and more fully together, without muddying those spaces with business agendas and organizational politics.

In this way, Holacracy creates a healthy separation of domains that are often fused in traditional organizations and sometimes even more so in progressive organizations. My business partner Tom Thomison describes this as differentiating the "personal space" and the "tribe space" from the "role space" and the "organizational space." I love this distinction, and what it points to. These very different spheres of human experience often get blurred, because they all coexist within any organization. The personal and tribe spaces are where all the wonderful richness of being human comes into play; the former is about you and your values, passions, talents, ambitions, and identity, while the latter is about how we interact and our shared values, culture, meaning making, and language. The role space, on the other hand, is where we take action *in role*, as the role's steward, in order to express its purpose and enact its accountabilities. Finally, the organizational space is the result of working together role to role and governing those roles for the sake of the organization's purpose.

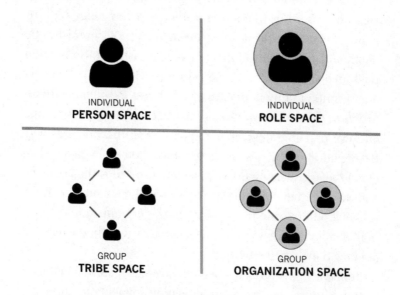

Done well, Holacracy doesn't devalue the personal and interpersonal domains, as some people fear at first—in fact, I regularly see it instill a deeper honoring of the personal, much more even than I've seen in many organizations that focus entirely on those dimensions. It does so by clearly differentiating these four spaces and holding appropriate boundaries between them. This allows all the spaces to coexist without any one dominating the others, and it shifts them from unconscious fusion and blurred boundaries to a healthy marriage, distinct yet integrated.

With all of Holacracy's processes focusing on the role-to-role

and organizational spaces—and not much else—our interpersonal tribe space is left in a rather notable state of anarchy.
An organization can create apps to regulate this space when
doing so is truly useful for the organization's purpose; however,
I believe there's something quite powerful about leaving this
space as unregulated as is practical, at least by the organization. If two or more people wish to agree to something—to communicate more empathetically, for example—they have every
right to do so. But when organizational policy today requires
people to do so for the sake of getting results, it diminishes the
depth and authenticity of that potential agreement. Rather than
push people to relate in a certain way, Holacracy allows the
organization to function optimally *however we humans decide
to relate to one another personally*. It resists efforts to fuse
our own personal development goals or cultural desires with
the organization's needs and governance. It keeps human values
out of the organizational space, which also keeps the organization out of our human-value space. And, perhaps more important,
it keeps others who are working in the organizational space
from dominating us with their own human values in the name of
organizational productivity.

Ironically, this turns out to be the best recipe I've found for a
human culture that has more empathy, connection, authentic
communication, and whatever other generative human dynamics we might seek. These are free to emerge naturally when we
can work together to care for another entity (the organization)
and its purpose, in a clear space, free of the pressure to appear
as others believe we should—unless we've consciously agreed
to do so.

This foundation really does create a new world at work, a
world in which you have the space and autonomy to do what
you need to do in order to fulfill your roles, without any requirement to get consensus or buy-in from anyone. And a world

where the authority you hold can't be co-opted by a group process just because someone doesn't like the specific decisions you make. You know who is accountable for what, and what you have the right to expect from others (and vice versa), so you don't have to navigate the bureaucracy, politics, and ego that come with implicit expectations. And when something is unclear, or when authorities or expectations need to evolve, there is an integrative governance process to generate that clarity. Imagine going to work each morning and showing up authentically in service of something larger than yourself, unburdened by others' implicit ideas about how you should behave or what's expected of you, and then leaving work most days feeling that your capacities have been well used that day, your gifts harnessed and integrated for a purpose you choose to serve. I love this new world that Holacracy has created in my organization—and the way it has liberated the other spaces in my life as well. Once you get over the initial unfamiliarity that comes from doing things differently than you've ever done them before, and once you adjust to the new control system, you may find yourself pleasantly surprised by how smoothly and freely you and your organization can move through the unpredictable and fast-changing terrain in which we all find ourselves today.

The Evolution of Organization

Many of the shifts I've explored in this chapter are not unique to Holacracy. Holacracy is just one example of a system that uses peer-to-peer self-organization and distributed control in lieu of more traditional approaches to achieving order. While I think it's novel in many ways, you don't have to look far to find other systems and processes that reflect a similar paradigm. In fact, I believe Holacracy is just one expression of a broader evolution toward a new way of structuring our world and our interactions, and I hope it can help with that larger shift. At the least, I think Holacracy can serve as an example that order doesn't require top-down rulers. I see people habitually giving up their autonomy to leaders of various sorts in the world today, and that's not surprising. Most of us grew up in households with patriarchal authority figures, then went to work in an environment structured much the same way, and perhaps became those authority figures ourselves, either at work or as parents. That socially ingrained pattern repeats and reinforces itself in so many aspects of our lives.

Organizations running with Holacracy create the potential for those within to have a very different experience—one in which power is distributed and we all get to be adults together. Where our sovereignty is honored and there are no ultimate authority figures to look up to, where there's just us, supporting each other as well as we can while we each lead our parts of the system. I hope that experience helps trigger deeper questions and perhaps some skepticism when leaders and authority figures of all sorts urge us to trust them and their use of power over our lives and others'.

One way or another, in both organizations and society, I think we'll continue to see static, centralized control systems giving way to something else. Evolution seems to favor processes that allow peer-to-peer, emergent order to show up in response to real tensions. I think one of the best ways we can enable that is to infuse governance throughout a system—a process so fully integrated that it just happens, like breathing, with no need for master architects to apply a perfect design up front. And there's a beautiful paradox here: when you have a system that distributes authority and honors the autonomy of all of its parts and players, you also get a system capable of acting more as a cohesive, integrated whole at the same time. So we needn't actually choose between centralized and distributed systems. The beauty of a functioning holarchy is that it gives us both—autonomous whole entities, made of interconnected parts that themselves are autonomous and whole, at every level of scale.

Finally, if there's one thing evolution favors most of all, perhaps it's evolution itself. Evolution's wheels of design have been turning since the beginning of time, searching out novel structures of ever greater depth and complexity. With each innovative leap, evolution seems to find ways to increase the speed of the evolutionary process itself, and to extend its reach into more and more domains of life. Ultimately, Holacracy is an invitation to consciously engage with that process in a new way, using a new tool. Because whether via Holacracy or another system, evolution will find its way into our organizations. It's just a matter of time. We can steward it in, or we can fight it for a while—but one way or another, evolution will have its way with us.

NOTES

1. David Packard, *The HP Way: How Bill and I Built Our Company* (HarperBusiness, 2006), p. 142.
2. Eric Beinhocker, *The Origin of Wealth: The Radical Remaking of Economics and What It Means for Business and Society* (Harvard Business Review Press, 2007), p. 12.
3. Ibid., p. 334.
4. Gary Hamel, speech at the 2009 World Business Forum. Quoted in Seth Kahan, "Time for Management 2.0," *Fast Company*, October 6, 2009, http://www.fastcompany.com/blog/seth-kahan/leading-change /hamel-hypercritical-change-points-radical-changes-required -management.
5. Gary Hamel, "First, Let's Fire All the Managers," *Harvard Business Review*, December 2011, https://hbr.org/2011/12/first-lets-fire-all -the-managers, accessed December 2014.
6. Alexis Gonzales-Black's remarks are drawn from the Zappos Insights blog post "What Does Leadership in Self-Organization Look Like?," October 8, 2014, http://www.zapposinsights.com/blog/item/what -does-leadership-in-selforganization-look-like, accessed October 2014; and Alexis Gonzales-Black, "Holacracy at Zappos—The First Year of Adoption," online interview by Anna McGrath, October 29, 2014.
7. Evan Williams, speaking at the 2013 Wisdom 2.0 conference.
8. David Allen, GTD Times Podcast, "What If We All Had Account-ability?," September 2011.
9. Michael Gerber, *The E-Myth Revisited* (HarperCollins, 2004), pp. 97–115.

10. David Allen, *Making It All Work: Winning at the Game of Work and the Business of Life* (Penguin Books, 2009).

11. David Allen, *Getting Things Done: The Art of Stress-Free Productivity* (Penguin Books, 2002), p. 38.

12. David Allen, "Productive Living" newsletter, http://gettingthingsdone.com/newsletters/archive/0713.html, July 18, 2013.

13. Nassim Nicholas Taleb, *The Black Swan: The Impact of the Highly Improbable* (Random House, 2007), p. 157.

14. Beinhocker, *Origin of Wealth*, p. 347.

15. Ibid., p. 14.

16. Gonzales-Black, "Holacracy at Zappos."

ACKNOWLEDGMENTS

Many people have contributed to Holacracy, whether through direct effort to pioneer the method and its use in the world, or indirectly, through their own work that influenced Holacracy's development. It's difficult to list and pay homage to all of these sources of help and inspiration, so, with advance apologies to those I know I'll miss, I'd like to acknowledge and thank whom I can in these final pages.

For the exquisite clarity and utility of his Getting Things Done method, not to mention for embracing Holacracy in its early days and writing an awesome foreword to this book, a very special thanks to David Allen. GTD is a shining example of the kind of system I was seeking with Holacracy—an inevitable discovery and codification of the most natural means to process, organize, and respond to the many inputs from our world. I sought the same kind of "natural laws" of collective organization that GTD offered for individual organization, and David's work was a source of significant inspiration, in addition to its more direct contributions to Holacracy's vernacular and its key concepts.

For catalyzing and pushing me in all the right ways, I'm particularly grateful to Tom Thomison, my cofounder of Holacracy-One. Tom served as a near-perfect foil for my own energy and focus; he challenged Holacracy in the early days in ways no one else had—his friendly agitation forced needed development and clarity in Holacracy's core rules and processes, and helped me differentiate myself from my creation. He was also instrumental in building HolacracyOne and pioneering much of what we now know about shifting organizations to Holacracy, and his boundless compassion and selfless service have been deeply nourishing and supportive to me and to so many others doing this work.

For joining HolacracyOne and helping express its purpose in the world, I'm grateful to all of my business partners for their energy, companionship, and continual hard work. I'd especially like to thank Alexia Bowers, who was with us from the start, as well as Karilen Mays, Olivier Compagne, and Deborah Boyar, who joined us early on and contributed immensely, in particular as our first Holacracy coaches beyond Tom and myself. Thanks also to Lewis Hoffman, partly for his deep contributions to our software development efforts, and even more because his openhearted presence has been a joy to work with and gives me something to aspire to. I'd also like to acknowledge our early licensees for their help spreading Holacracy in the world, especially Bernard Marie Chiquet, Diederick Janse, and Anna McGrath. A further tip of the hat goes to Dennis Wittrock, a key early advocate whose support enabled our first workshops in Europe.

For supporting my early exploration toward Holacracy at my software company, and for (mostly) putting up with me as I ruthlessly experimented on our business, I'm grateful to my cofounders Anthony Moquin and Alexia Bowers, and to our more process-focused agile software developers, Bill Schofield and Gareth Powell. Everyone who worked there over the years deserves credit, too, as the constant experimentation that eventually led to an elegant system was often not elegant itself.

For their books and other work that played a key role in my own journey toward improving organizations, thanks to: Linda Berens, Barry Oshry, Peter Senge, Patrick Lencioni, Jim Collins, and Elliott Jaques.

For their unique models and perspectives, which ultimately helped me make sense of the system I was building and what worked about it, I'd like to acknowledge the works of: Eric Beinhocker, Nassim Nicholas Taleb, Ken Wilber, Murray Rothbard, and Ludwig von Mises.

For all their contributions to self-organization, agile planning, and the mind-set shifts that go with them, thanks to the many pioneers in the agile software development community, including Kent Beck, Mary Poppendieck, Ken Schwaber, Jeff Sutherland, and Mike Cohn, among others.

For his work with sociocracy and books on the same, I'm appreciative of Gerard Endenburg. His system informed Holacracy's early development and inspired its use of rep links and its election process.

For helping with this book, I'm in debt to my writing consultant, Ellen Daly; without her significant effort and skill, these pages might never have seen the light of day. I owe much to my editor, Will Schwalbe, who, along with my agent, Lisa Queen, saw more potential in this book than even I did, and helped me see just what this manuscript needed to achieve it. Perhaps more important, they knew what to leave out. Thanks also to Chris Cowan, who led much of the effort within HolacracyOne to get this book to market, and to the entire team at Henry Holt who helped steward us through the journey, especially Maggie Richards and Pat Eisenmann.

For supporting my very unconventional childhood and helping me build such a solid sense of self throughout, I'm grateful to my mother, Shirley Mackey—if she hadn't done such a great job of catalyzing the development of my strong and healthy ego,

I wouldn't have needed a system capable of protecting others from it.

For contributing to my own development and to Holacracy's, in ways I'm still regularly discovering and know I can't possibly capture with the crude and limited tool of language, my heart and my gratitude go to my wife, Alexia Bowers. Her name has already appeared twice above for her more tangible and easily honored contributions, although they barely scratch the surface of the many ways she's contributed to the story of Holacracy, and directly to the writing of this book.

Finally, for their courage, vision, adaptability, and discipline, I offer a deep bow to all of the leaders and companies referenced in this book and the many others practicing Holacracy day to day. They are part of pioneering a new way of organizing and working together in the world, and in the process they're helping Holacracy outgrow my own direct stewardship and become a true movement. I know Holacracy's future evolution will be driven more and more by this larger user community and the tensions they sense about the system itself, rather than through my own direct tinkering. Like a parent watching a child leave home to start her own family, I'm especially grateful to see this creation I birthed finding such a supportive and engaged community, so Holacracy can do its own life's work in the world, whatever that may turn out to be.

INDEX

Page numbers in *italics* refer to illustrations.

ABOUT THE AUTHOR

BRIAN J. ROBERTSON developed Holacracy while experimenting with management techniques within his own companies, originally as a CEO. He previously founded and led a fast-growth software company, and he now works with HolacracyOne, the organization he launched to support Holacracy. His efforts have helped hundreds of companies around the world install and practice the method. He lives near Philadelphia.